Twice Yours

A Parable
of God's Gift

Twice Yours

A Parable of God's Gift

Written by Nan Gurley
Illustrated by Bill Farnsworth

Zonderkidz

Twice Yours
Copyright © 2001 by Nan Gurley
Illustrations copyright © 2001 by Bill Farnsworth
Requests for information should be addressed to:

Zonder**kidz**™

The children's group of Zondervan
Grand Rapids, Michigan 49530
www.zonderkidz.com

Zonderkidz is a trademark of Zondervan.

ISBN: 0-310-70194-5

Scripture quotations are from HOLY BIBLE, NEW
INTERNATIONAL READER'S VERSION® Copyright ©
1995, 1996, 1998 by International Bible Society. Used by
permission of Zondervan. All rights reserved.

Editor: Gwen Ellis
Art direction and design: Michelle Lenger

Printed in Singapore
01 02 03 04 / TP / 5 4 3 2 1

This one is for my brothers
Chip, Cris, and Tim . . .
for all we were,
for all we are becoming.

- n.g. -

To my wife Deborah
and my daughters,
Allison and Caitlin.

- b.f. -

"What are you carving, Grandpa?" Cory asked as he climbed onto the porch swing and sat beside his grandfather.

"Something for you."

*F*or me? What is it?"

"Something to help you remember who you are."

Cory watched his grandfather's hands. They were big and brown and they knew just what to do with a piece of wood and a pocketknife.

"This piece of wood reminds me of something that happened a long time ago– I was about your age."

"Tell me, Grandpa. Tell me a story!" Cory leaned back against Grandpa's shoulder and waited for him to begin.

For weeks a boy worked to make a lovely little sailboat. Carefully he carved the boat out of balsa wood, forming the bow, the stern, the hull, and the rudder. Then he searched through scraps of material his mother had given him until he found the perfect fabric to make the sail.

"When every piece was put together and the paint and glue were finally dry, the boy cut a long piece of string and tied it to the back of the boat.

"After school the next day, the boy hurried home. Gently he picked up his sailboat and ran down the road to the stream that flowed through the town.

Kneeling at the edge of the creek, the boy placed his sailboat in the water. Holding the end of the string tightly in his hand, he pushed the boat out toward the middle of the stream. The boat floated out, away from the bank, away from the boy. When it reached the middle of the stream, it was pulled into the fast-moving current. The boy watched with joy as the boat sailed over rocks and past the roots of trees. 'We're sailing!' he cried, running along beside his homemade boat.

Every day the boy came back to the creek and sailed his boat and pulled it back to shore, and sailed his boat and pulled it back to shore.

"One day when the boy was running along the stream bank beside his homemade sailboat, the string broke. 'Wait! Stop! Come back, little boat,' he cried, but the boat just sailed on down the stream and out of sight.

"Every day the boy walked up and down the creek bank searching for his boat. He was hoping that maybe it had washed up onto the bank or perhaps had become stuck behind a rock.

One day while searching for his beloved boat, the boy went farther downstream than he ever had before. He followed the creek through a grove of pine trees and under a footbridge. Suddenly, he saw up ahead a little boy playing with a boat. When he got closer he saw that it was his own homemade boat. The paint was chipped and the sail was torn, but still he recognized it as his own.

That's mine!' he shouted, running up to the other boy and reaching to grab the boat out of his hands.

"'No, it's not. It's mine. I found it.'

"'No! It's mine! I made it, but I lost it. Now give it back.'

"'Finders keepers, losers weepers!' said the other boy, still holding tightly to the boat.

"'I'll trade you for it.'

"'What do you have?'

The boy reached inside his pockets and pulled out everything he had. 'I have some string, two bottle caps, three marbles, a rubber snake, and a pocketknife.'

"'Well,' said the other boy, 'how much of that will you give me for the sailboat?'

'I'll give you everything I have,' the boy replied. 'You can have it all!'

"'It's a deal!' exclaimed the other boy, dropping the sailboat and reaching for the string, the bottle caps, the marbles, the rubber snake, and the pocketknife.

The boy picked up his sailboat and walked back upstream under the footbridge, through the grove of pine trees, and back to the place where he had first launched his sailboat. 'You're twice mine,' he said, hugging the boat tightly to his chest. 'Once because I made you, and once because I bought you.'"

Grandpa finished the story and whittled the last piece from his block of wood. Then he handed the carving to Cory. It was a cross.

"This is for you, Cory. It will remind you of the One who made you and then bought you."

What do you mean, Grandpa?"

"Jesus wanted you for his own. He created you to bring him joy, and then he paid for you–not with marbles and bottle caps and a pocketknife, but with something far more precious. He gave everything he had. He paid for you with his life."

Cory clutched the cross in his hands. "Thank you, Grandpa. That's the best story ever!"

Grandpa closed his knife and put it in his pocket. "Yes, it is, Cory. Indeed, it is."

You know that you were not bought with things that can pass away, like silver or gold. Instead, you were bought by the priceless blood of Christ…He was chosen before God created the world. But he came into the world in these last days for you.

1 Peter 1:18-20

114

VINCENT VAN GOGH

Wheatfields after the Rain (The Plain of Auvers),
1890
Oil on canvas, 73.3 × 92.4 cm
Carnegie Museum of Art, Pittsburgh, acquired
through the generosity of the Sarah Mellon Scaife
Family, 68.18

115
VINCENT VAN GOGH
Wheatfields with Reaper, Auvers, 1890
Oil on canvas, 73.6 × 93 cm
Toledo Museum of Art, Toledo, Ohio purchased with
funds from the Libbey Endowment, gift of Edward
Drummond Libbey, 1935.4

116
VINCENT VAN GOGH
Wheatfield with Cornflowers, 1890
Oil on canvas, 60 × 81 cm
Fondation Beyeler, Riehen / Basel, Beyeler
collection

117 (pp. 122–3)
VINCENT VAN GOGH
Rain – Auvers, 1890
Oil on canvas, 50.3 × 100.2 cm
Amgueddfa Cymru – National Museum Wales

top of the canvas. In *Landscape at Twilight* (fig. 118) Van Gogh captured the scene as dusk fell, a time of day so often painted by Daubigny. He described the melancholy, poetic landscape as 'a night effect – two completely dark pear trees against yellowing sky with wheatfields, and in the violet background the castle encased in the dark greenery.'[40] The track that cuts through the fields and draws the viewer into the scene is a tried and tested device that Daubigny used in his *Harvest* in 1851 (fig. 119) and Pissarro in his *La Varenne-Saint-Hilaire* (fig. 120); Van Gogh used it, too, in his famous *Wheatfield with Crows* (Van Gogh Museum, Amsterdam).

Among the last works he painted on 'double-square' canvases were two views of *Daubigny's Garden*. He had been thinking about this painting ever since he arrived in Auvers, as he wrote to Theo when he had finished the first version (fig. 123).[41] He had discovered when he arrived in the village that the artist's widow still lived there, and must immediately have conceived a plan to visit her. Madame Daubigny had been living in a villa in the centre of the village

since 1886. Daubigny had bought the house in 1877 but reportedly never lived or worked there, preferring his first studio.[42] Madame Daubigny gave Van Gogh permission to work in the garden and in mid-June he made a study (fig. 122) as the initial idea for 'a more important canvas of *Daubigny's* house and garden'.[43] By then he had run through his entire stock of canvas, so he painted it on a tea towel measuring 50 × 50 cm, exactly half a double square. In this first exploration of the subject he zoomed in on the flower bed in the garden; the house is largely hidden by the trees. In the large canvas he painted a few weeks later he showed the whole of the house and a bigger section of the garden, with Madame Daubigny in the background and a black cat in the foreground (fig. 123). He then painted another version the same size, which he gave to the widow (now in the Hiroshima Museum of Art). The three paintings of Daubigny's garden were his homage to the artist he had admired all his life and who had given him new inspiration in Auvers. In his last letter to Theo, written on 23 July, he made a sketch of the second

118
VINCENT VAN GOGH
Landscape at Twilight, 1890
Oil on canvas, 50.2 × 101 cm
Van Gogh Museum, Amsterdam
(Vincent van Gogh Foundation)

119
CHARLES FRANÇOIS DAUBIGNY
The Harvest, 1851
Oil on canvas, 135 × 196 cm
Musée d'Orsay, Paris

120
CAMILLE PISSARRO
La Varenne-Saint-Hilaire, 1863
Oil on canvas, 49.6 × 74 cm
Museum of Fine Arts, Budapest

123
VINCENT VAN GOGH
Daubigny's Garden, 1890
Oil on canvas, 50 × 101.5 cm
Collection Rudolf Staechelin

version and described the painting, which he called 'one of my most deliberate canvases' (fig. 121).[44] In the same letter he enclosed four more sketches of paintings of thatched roofs and wheatfields, among them *Wheatfields after the Rain (The Plain of Auvers)* (fig. 114). Despite the solace he derived from nature he was gloomy and concerned about the future. On 27 July he shot himself in the chest. He died of his injuries two days later and was buried in the cemetery bordering the wheatfields in Auvers.

Van Gogh's life ended in the village where Daubigny had spent his last years, placing him literally in the footsteps of the French painter. The paintings of Daubigny and the Barbizon artists had strongly influenced Van Gogh's perception of the landscape around him and had helped to shape his view of nature. Daubigny had imbued his landscapes with personal feelings, and this was exactly what Van Gogh strove for in his work. In his landscape paintings he wanted to express the emotions that nature evoked in him, to 'tell you what I can't say in words, what I consider healthy and fortifying about the countryside', as he wrote in Auvers.[45] That he succeeded in this is clear from the acclaim that his work started to receive soon after his death. *Wheatfield under Troubled Skies* and *Wheatfield with Crows* have become iconic works of art, precisely because of the strong feelings they inspire in the viewer. And just as Daubigny had been a guiding light for Van Gogh, he himself provided inspiration for generations of artists to come.

le jardin de Daubigny

'Tout dans son talent est prime-sautier, sain, ouvert':[1] Observations on Daubigny's Late Painting Techniques

René Boitelle

Charles François Daubigny's depictions of rural France occupy an important place in the development of nineteenth-century landscape painting. The artist's prolific output, his commercial success and standing in the Parisian art scene, from the 1850s until his death in 1878, underline his significance in the history of the genre. Yet critical response to his works during the second half of his career was often mixed. On occasion his technique was labelled unsound, his application of paint crude, and his lack of finish inappropriate. Théophile Gautier stated that Daubigny did not finish his work properly and that he seemed to be satisfied with presenting mere unfinished works and 'impressions'.[2] Nowadays these aspects of Daubigny's later paintings are highly valued, since they are often perceived as being associated with the early stages of Impressionism.

Although Daubigny's painting techniques are often considered key to his artistic output, little is still known about his studio practice. Only a small number of recent studies on individual pictures dating from different periods of his career are available, and these have yielded much relevant data that contributes to our understanding of how these paintings were created.[3] This essay presents some of the findings of technical research performed on Daubigny's later paintings (early 1860s to about 1875) in The Mesdag Collection,[4] as well as several relevant works from other collections.

Painting Supports: Convention and Originality

In the course of the nineteenth century a wide range of standard-sized supports became available to painters. Dozens of artist's materials shops in business in Paris during Daubigny's lifetime offered for sale pre-stretched canvases and panels or boards in fixed sizes (denoted by numbers) and formats (*portrait*, *paysage* or *marine*).[5] These pre-manufactured supports were already covered with grounds and, in the cases of canvases, were on standard-sized stretchers (fig. 127). The grounds on canvases had been either applied after stretching by the colourman, or (as was often the case) the canvas had been cut from a large roll of prepared fabric to match a specific size of stretcher. For reasons of economy and/or artistic preference, it was also possible to buy any length of unprepared canvas from a roll, which could be stretched in the studio. In this case, artists could

DETAIL fig. 134
CHARLES FRANÇOIS DAUBIGNY
Towpath on the Banks of the Oise, c. 1875

use an empty standard-size stretcher lying around in the studio or assemble loose stretcher bars to form a new, non-standard stretcher to suit their ultimate aim.[6] All this potential variety is relevant to any discussion of a painter's oeuvre as decisions about the size and nature of a support (square, rectangular, horizontal, canvas, wooden, prepared or unprepared, etc.) are intimately linked to the composition, execution, finish and presentation of the paintings.

In many respects Daubigny fits the accepted practice of his time in his choice of supports and other materials, and like his contemporaries he seems to have turned to a whole range of suppliers over the course of his career, either the well-known shops in Paris or unidentified ones in the towns he visited while travelling. It appears he did not favour one particular colourman, but bought his materials at different shops during the same period. Standard-sized and commercially prepared canvases can be found throughout Daubigny's oeuvre, as well as panels with or without a ground that came straight from a colourman's shop. However, recent examination of three of his works reveals some unconventional choices in the artist's use of supports

during the later years of his career. These include the readjustment of supports before, during or after the painting process, and a preference for non-standard canvases, as well as the vigorous application of his own ground layers.

Daubigny's *Banks of the Oise* (fig. 124), painted in 1872, illustrates his practice of modifying the size of a commercially prepared support before the painting process. The wooden support of this oil sketch, with its stippled cream white ground, was in all probability manufactured by the firm of Alexis Ottoz, whose stamp can be seen on the reverse of the panel.[7] A pencil line can be made out on the ground layer at the left edge. This was drawn with a ruler to mark where the original panel was to be sawn to reduce it in size (fig. 125). The stamp, traditionally positioned in the middle of the panel and in line with the originally intended direction of the support, is now visible at the top right corner and turned 90 degrees to the right (fig. 126). Apparently Daubigny had decided to alter a fully prepared panel to a suitable format before taking it outside to paint this twilight river scene.

An example of an adjustment carried out before the completion of the painting process can be found

124
CHARLES FRANÇOIS DAUBIGNY
Banks of the Oise, 1872
Oil on panel, 34.7 × 58.3 cm
The Mesdag Collection, The Hague

125
CHARLES FRANÇOIS DAUBIGNY
Banks of the Oise, 1872
Detail of fig. 124

126
CHARLES FRANÇOIS DAUBIGNY
Banks of the Oise, 1872
Detail of the reverse side of fig. 124

127
List of standard-size pre-stretched canvases available in mid-nineteenth-century Paris Lefranc et Cie, *Fabrique de couleurs et vernis. Toiles à peindre* […], 1855

128
CHARLES FRANÇOIS DAUBIGNY
Sunset near Villerville, c. 1876
Fig. 129 with lines indicating the position of the first set of crossbars

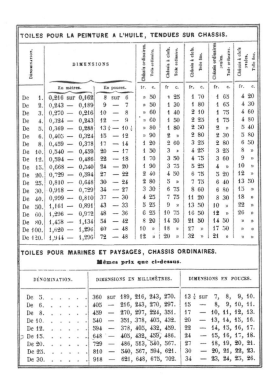

TOILES POUR LA PEINTURE A L'HUILE, TENDUES SUR CHASSIS.

Dénomination.	DIMENSIONS				Châssis ordinaires. Toile ordinaire.	Châssis à clefs. Toile ordinaire.	Châssis à clefs. Toile fine.	Châssis ordinaires. Toile ordinaire.	Châssis à clefs. Toiles, Toile fine.
	En mètres.		En pouces.		fr. c.	fr. c.	fr. c.	fr. c.	fr. c.
De 1.	0,216 sur	0,162	8 sur	6	» 50	» 25	1 70	1 65	4 20
De 2.	0,243 —	0,189	9 —	7	» 50	1 30	1 80	1 65	4 30
De 3.	0,270 —	0,216	10 —	8	» 60	1 40	2 10	1 75	4 60
De 4.	0,324 —	0,243	12 —	9	» 60	1 50	2 25	1 75	4 80
De 5.	0,369 —	0,288	13½ — 10½		» 80	1 80	2 30	2 »	5 40
De 6.	0,405 —	0,324	15 —	12	» 90	2 »	2 80	2 30	5 80
De 8.	0,459 —	0,378	17 —	14	1 20	2 60	3 25	2 80	6 50
De 10.	0,540 —	0,459	20 —	17	1 50	3 »	4 25	3 25	8 »
De 12.	0,594 —	0,486	22 —	18	1 70	3 50	4 75	3 60	9 »
De 15.	0,668 —	0,540	24 —	20	1 90	3 75	5 25	4 »	10 »
De 20.	0,729 —	0,594	27 —	22	2 40	4 50	6 75	5 20	12 »
De 25.	0,810 —	0,648	30 —	24	2 80	5 »	7 75	6 40	13 50
De 30.	0,918 —	0,729	34 —	27	3 30	6 75	8 60	6 80	15 »
De 40.	0,999 —	0,810	37 —	30	4 25	7 75	11 20	8 30	18 »
De 50.	1,161 —	0,891	43 —	33	5 25	9 »	13 50	10 »	22 »
De 60.	1,296 —	0,972	48 —	36	6 25	10 75	16 50	12 »	26 »
De 80.	1,458 —	1,134	54 —	42	8 20	14 50	21 50	14 50	» »
De 100.	1,620 —	1,296	60 —	48	10 »	18 »	27 »	17 50	» »
De 120.	1,944 —	1,296	72 —	48	12 »	20 »	32 »	21 »	» »

TOILES POUR MARINES ET PAYSAGES, CHASSIS ORDINAIRES.

Mêmes prix que ci-dessus.

DÉNOMINATION.	DIMENSIONS EN MILLIMÈTRES.	DIMENSIONS EN POUCES.
De 5.	360 sur 189, 216, 243, 270.	13½ sur 7, 8, 9, 10.
De 6.	405 — 216, 243, 270, 297.	15 — 8, 9, 10, 11.
De 8.	459 — 270, 297, 224, 351.	17 — 10, 11, 12, 13.
De 10.	540 — 351, 378, 405, 432.	20 — 13, 14, 15, 16.
De 12.	594 — 378, 405, 432, 459.	22 — 14, 15, 16, 17.
De 15.	648 — 405, 432, 459, 486.	24 — 15, 16, 17, 18.
De 20.	729 — 486, 513, 540, 567.	27 — 18, 19, 20, 21.
De 25.	810 — 540, 567, 594, 621.	30 — 20, 21, 22, 23.
De 30.	918 — 621, 648, 675, 702.	34 — 23, 24, 25, 26.

129
CHARLES FRANÇOIS DAUBIGNY
Sunset near Villerville, c. 1876
Oil on canvas, 89 × 130 cm
The Mesdag Collection, The Hague

on *Sunset near Villerville* (fig. 129). The work dates from the final years of the artist's career and its present dimensions match a standard-size *paysage* no. 60.[8] However, close inspection of the paint surface indicates that Daubigny reduced the size of the canvas. Two sets of fine cracks running in parallel lines betray the original position of the stretcher's crossbars before the canvas was made smaller. In a stretcher of this size the crossbars would have been placed symmetrically, but the location of the cracks does not relate to the present crossbars (fig. 128). Furthermore, parts of the painted composition (beach, sea and sky) extend over the top left and right edges of the canvas. All this suggests that the support was originally much bigger and must initially have been attached to a larger stretcher. Daubigny, at some point during the painting process, decided to reduce its size and stretch it onto its current stretcher.[9]

Daubigny's oeuvre contains many large canvases, with a noticeable increase in their number after 1872. Some of them are of a standard size, but it appears that he also decided to devise new formats that were better suited to his artistic ambitions and inspired by the landscapes he was painting. In this he showed himself to be unconventional, compared to most of his contemporaries who painted their landscapes mainly on standard-size canvases. The dimensions of these custom-designed canvases were adapted from standard-size stretchers. For example, the height of *Sunset at Villerville* (fig. 130)[10] matches that of a *portrait* no. 40 or *paysage* no. 50, but its width is derived from a *portrait* or *paysage* no. 80 stretcher.

In 1854, Daubigny made the first of many visits to Villerville, a small village on the Normandy coast. His boundless enthusiasm for the place ignited his inspiration. In a letter to Geoffroy-Dechaume, he wrote

130
CHARLES FRANÇOIS DAUBIGNY
Sunset at Villerville, 1874
Oil on canvas, 84 × 147 cm
The Mesdag Collection, The Hague

131 (pp. 138–9)
CHARLES FRANÇOIS DAUBIGNY
Cliffs near Villerville, 1864–72
Oil on canvas, 100 × 200 cm
The Mesdag Collection, The Hague

that the sunsets there made those of the celebrated seventeenth-century master Claude Lorrain appear dull by comparison, and stated that he would need large canvases to capture all that he saw.[11] At the time such a predilection for grand-scale canvases for landscapes made on the spot was still highly unusual, but in the years that followed Daubigny would increasingly paint on large canvases. If a painting could not be finished in front of the motif he would bring it back to his studio to be completed or reworked at a later stage. In another letter to Henriet written just after returning home from a later campaign in the country (1872), Daubigny confessed to having made 55 *pochades*, 'one of 3 metres and four of 2 metres'.[12] Whether he set these up outside in front of the motif or in the more sheltered surroundings of a temporary studio is of less significance than the fact that these sketches were made on monumental formats, which were traditionally reserved for highly finished and ambitious Salon paintings.

Of the large paintings from the second half of Daubigny's career one particular type, also non-standard, stands out: landscapes with a width about twice their height, or double-square canvases. These double squares were particularly suited to panoramic views of the sea, rivers and fields. An early example is *Villerville Seen from Le Ratier* (fig. 75), which originated from one of the artist's first visits to the Normandy coast in 1855.[13] As the years progressed, so too did his use of this particular format, with a marked increase between 1871 and 1877. Examples include the numerous versions of *Sunset at Villerville* (fig. 130), *Cliffs near Villerville* (fig. 131) and *The House of Mère Bazot, Valmondois* (fig. 132), as well as individual compositions such as the unfinished *Towpath on the Banks of the Oise* (fig. 134). On rare

occasions Daubigny turned the double-square format on its side, as in depictions of the *Ru de Valmondois*, where it enabled him to explore the effect of dark masses of foliage around narrow patches of light reflected in the small brook. Such was the appeal of this double-square format for landscape that some years later it was also chosen by Camille Pissarro for some of his views of the Oise valley and Vincent van Gogh in his depictions of the wheatfields near Auvers-sur-Oise and *Daubigny's Garden*.

Daubigny's tendency to experiment was not limited to the format of his supports. Examination of paintings from the second half of his career has shown that ground layers on many of the non-standard stretched canvases were applied in a lively and irregular manner with a palette knife after the canvases had been secured onto their stretchers. Alongside his preference for non-standard formats, Daubigny also developed a habit for making and applying his own ground layers.[14] Commercially prepared grounds applied with either palette knife or brushes usually have even surfaces, in various degrees of smoothness depending on the composition of the ground material, the number and thickness of the layers and the coarseness of the fabric covered by the ground. In contrast, the somewhat crude and irregular textures of the opaque, off-white ground layers in later Daubigny canvases are characterised by unevenness, flat areas bordered by ridges of excess ground material and straight or curved scratches, all of which are indicative of the vigorous use of a palette knife.[15] X-radiographs of paintings such as *Cliffs near Villerville* (fig. 133) and *Moonlight* (figs 135 & 136)[16] confirm the impression the textured surface renders to the naked eye. The swiftness and force with which the ground material

has been applied, in a manner quite unlike the traditional manufacturer's practice, becomes clearly visible. In some areas large losses in ground and underlying paint layers can be observed, which were never filled but instead left to dry before painting continued (fig. 137). As these textures remained completely or partially visible after being covered by successive paint layers, it can be concluded that Daubigny did not mind these irregularities and that he may even have developed a preference for such surface effects.

The Painting Process: Reworking and Reusing

By around 1860 Daubigny had developed a more open, looser approach to the concept of finish in his paintings. He had, in effect, challenged the traditional notions of preparatory work, embodied in widely used terms such as *dessin*, *étude*, *esquisse*, *pochade* and their relation to the eventual *tableau fini*. From then on he developed the practice of making continual adjustments to his works, even those on a large scale, and often after he had added his signature.[17]

Pentimenti (additions and revisions) were a recurring feature of Daubigny's landscape paintings. Small works begun *en plein air* in front of the motif were sometimes finished at a later stage by the addition of features such as a *repoussoir* (an object painted in the foreground of a composition in order

132
CHARLES FRANÇOIS DAUBIGNY
The House of Mère Bazot, Valmondois, c. 1874
Oil on canvas, 86.5 × 162.4 cm
The Mesdag Collection, The Hague

133
X-radiograph of Daubigny's *Cliffs near Villerville*
(fig. 131)
Courtesy J. Paul Getty Museum, Los Angeles

134
CHARLES FRANÇOIS DAUBIGNY
Towpath on the Banks of the Oise, c. 1875
Oil on canvas, 89 × 184 cm
The Mesdag Collection, The Hague

135
X-radiograph of Daubigny's *Moonlight* (fig. 136),
showing that the ground material was applied
quickly in parallel and crossing strokes
Courtesy R. Gerritsen, Amsterdam

136
CHARLES FRANÇOIS DAUBIGNY
Moonlight, c. 1875
Oil on canvas, 65 × 48.8 cm
The Mesdag Collection, The Hague

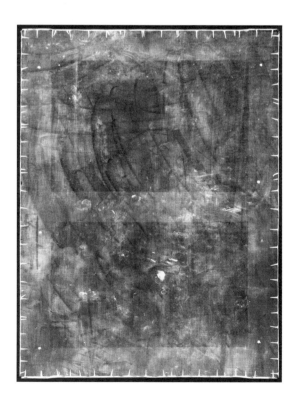

to direct the viewer's eye to the distance), a figure or brightly coloured highlights in the clouds. This can be observed in the *Beach at Ebb Tide* (fig. 138). More often than not the position of the horizon was lowered, or the contours of trees and shrubs, first set down in earth colours or dull greens, were redefined and given a new shape by applying opaque colours in the sky area around them (figs 139 & 124). Even when a painting was already well underway Daubigny could still change his mind about the position of the sun or moon, often moving them only a few centimetres away from their initial location, suggesting he felt the exact placement of these celestial bodies was of great importance. This phenomenon can be observed, for example, among others in *Sunset at Villerville* (fig. 140) and *April Moon* (fig. 141).

On some occasions earlier work was overpainted completely with a new composition. X-radiography and analyses of paint cross sections from *Haystacks by Moonlight*, *c.* 1875 have shown that Daubigny painted this work over an earlier varnished portrait of his wife (figs 142 & 143).[18] Unsigned and painted in a sketchy, loose manner often associated with the final years of the artist's career, *Haystacks* is an essay in the effects of moonlight on the landscape, a phenomenon that particularly interested him in the 1870s.

Ambitious compositions in larger formats were not exempt from re-use or extensive change. Infrared reflectography of the unfinished *Towpath on the Banks of the Oise* (fig. 144)[19] revealed the presence of a completely different, equally unfinished composition underneath. In the latter, a farmhouse with a smoking chimney can be seen on the left side and, towards the upper right, a partially covered moon shines through clouds. This motif is linked to a night scene known from an illustration recording Daubigny's contribution to the Salon of 1865, as well as from two works on paper.[20]

More complex to decipher are those paintings he decided to rework partially, sometimes years later, resulting in significantly altered appearances. The impulse for such modifications often seems to have come from the artist himself (regardless of critical response) when he was preparing to send a 'finished' painting to an exhibition abroad. However, a *Moonrise* (fig. 79) painted on an ambitious scale (at that time unprecedented for Daubigny) met with such an unfavourable response at the Salon of 1868, that he reportedly felt forced to rework it extensively before sending it on to the Vienna Exposition Universelle in 1873.

A celebrated instance of Daubigny reworking a painting years after completion can be found in *Cliffs near Villerville*, first shown at the 1864 Salon. The realistic depiction of this seaside village was generally well reviewed. One critic wrote he could smell the salt

138
CHARLES FRANÇOIS DAUBIGNY
Beach at Ebb Tide, c. 1876
Oil on panel, 35 × 55 cm
Rijksmuseum, Amsterdam, gift of
M.C., Baroness van Lynden-van Pallandt,
The Hague

139 (left)
CHARLES FRANÇOIS DAUBIGNY
Towpath on the Banks of the Oise, c. 1875
Detail of fig. 134

140 (middle)
CHARLES FRANÇOIS DAUBIGNY
Sunset at Villerville, 1874
Detail of fig. 130 with the first and final positions
of the setting sun

141 (below)
CHARLES FRANÇOIS DAUBIGNY
April Moon, 1875 (detail with the first and final
positions of the full moon)
Oil on panel, 65 × 110 cm
The Mesdag Collection, The Hague

142 (right)
X-radiograph of Daubigny's *Haystacks by Moonlight*
(fig. 143). Note the relatively open character of the
woven support, which represents a poorer quality
fabric than the more densely and regularly woven
canvases Daubigny favoured later in his career.
Courtesy R. Gerritsen, Amsterdam

143 (far right)
CHARLES FRANÇOIS DAUBIGNY
Haystacks by Moonlight, c. 1875
Oil on canvas, 60 × 73.5 cm
The Mesdag Collection, The Hague

144 (opposite)
Infrared reflectography of Daubigny's *Towpath
on the Banks of the Oise* (fig. 134)
Courtesy J. Paul Getty Museum, Los Angeles

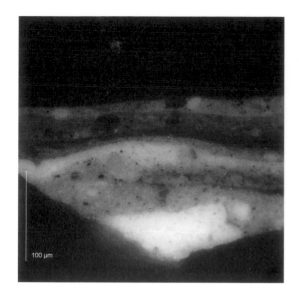

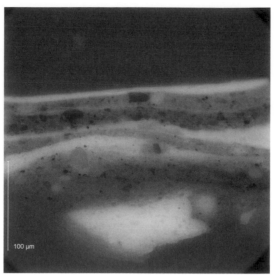

145
Paint cross section of Daubigny's *Cliffs near Villerville* (fig. 131) with crossed polarising filters, 50x objective. The paint cross section, taken from the middle of the painting at the slope of the dunes, shows a total of ten different paint and varnish layers. Note the distinct difference between the older series of blond pinkish layers at the bottom and the newer, darker ones painted on top $(1 \mu = 10^{-6} \text{ cm})$.
Courtesy A. Phenix, Getty Conservation Institute, Los Angeles

146
Paint cross section of Daubigny's *Cliffs near Villerville* (fig. 131) with UV fluorescence, 50x objective, the same section as fig. 145, showing the intermediate varnish layer.
Courtesy A. Phenix, Getty Conservation Institute, Los Angeles

air, another was moved by what he called the intimate and dynamic relationship between sky and earth, a third pronounced that Daubigny's talent had never before manifested itself so overwhelmingly and so assuredly. According to Henriet this painting was the first major composition that Daubigny painted entirely *en plein air*.[21]

Cross sections taken from different parts of the painting, especially those from the foreground, show two distinctly different sets of paint layers, separated from one another by a layer of varnish (figs 145 & 146). These confirm what can be detected on the paint surface. On top of the white-cream coloured ground, several thinner paint layers have been applied with an overall pinkish, beige and blond colour scheme. This light palette was later abandoned long after most of these layers had dried, when Daubigny later reworked the painting to create the surface now visible. Thicker, opaque layers of dark browns, greys and greens have been applied with a palette knife and brushes to create a darker *repoussoir* at the slope of the dunes in front of the village.

Close observation of the lower right corner around the present signature and date clearly reveals a fairly monochrome, brownish green patch of paint, that stands out and does not quite blend in with the rest of the foreground (fig. 147). Infrared reflectography of that area shows an earlier signature and date lying underneath the present one of *Daubigny 1872*. Surprisingly the date underneath is not 1864, but 1871 (fig. 148). Of course, this does not mean that a date of 1864 is not present at a lower level of the

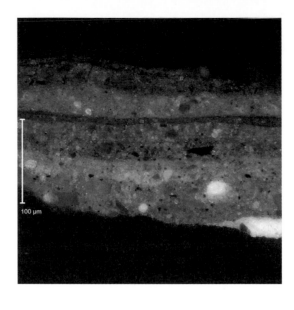

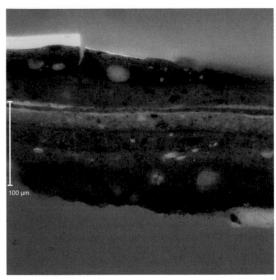

147
CHARLES FRANÇOIS DAUBIGNY
Cliffs near Villerville, 1864–72
detail of fig. 131

148
Infrared reflectography of Daubigny's *Cliffs near Villerville* (fig. 131) shows an earlier signature and date lying underneath.

149
Paint cross section of Daubigny's *Cliffs near Villerville* (fig. 131) with crossed polarising filters, 40x objective, showing fourteen different paint and varnish layers.
Courtesy A. Phenix, Getty Conservation Institute, Los Angeles

150
Paint cross section of Daubigny's *Cliffs near Villerville* (fig. 131) with UV fluorescence, 40x objective, the same section as fig. 149, showing two thin varnish layers with a thin paint layer in between.
Courtesy A. Phenix, Getty Conservation Institute, Los Angeles

paint stratigraphy. At this stage it remains impossible to delve deeper and verify the presence of the presumed earliest date of 1864. But this recently revealed date of 1871, hitherto unknown, adds a new chapter to the history of the painting's various reworkings by Daubigny.

Examination of one of the cross sections taken from the foreground seems to confirm the two reworkings the painting received after 1864. The intermediate varnish layer visible in one cross section between the first and later reworking consists in fact of two layers. A thin paint layer in between these two layers of varnish can be detected (figs 149 & 150). It is possible that it belongs to a first reworking, executed in 1871 during Daubigny's brief stay in Paris before he left for the Netherlands with his son Karl. This was then coated with a new, locally applied varnish layer, which in 1872 was covered by a more extensive reworking of the composition.

In his monograph on Daubigny, Henriet devoted an often-quoted passage to the creation of *Cliffs near Villerville*, mentioning that the artist secured the canvas at the sides to two stakes firmly planted in the ground, and that the canvas remained outdoors until it was finished. In spite of the risks posed by cows and the pranks of the local boys, the artist would wait for a favourable moment, then run back to the canvas as soon as the weather matched the original effect of nature he wish to capture.[22] The surface does show small areas of abrasion in the sky that were later reworked by the artist, either in 1864, 1871 or 1872. Dents and ridges can be seen in both the sky as well

as the landscape. However, none of this proves that there is any truth in Henriet's anecdote; the abrasions in the sky could easily have occurred when the painting was transported, and the dents and ridges visible in many spots of both sky and foreground are clearly the result of working with a palette knife, as can be seen in the X-radiograph. The position of these marks matches thicker passages of priming material. Clearly, Daubigny applied the ground with a palette knife in broad, sweeping movements across the entire surface, as described above.

Daubigny's choice of pigments would seem to be consistent with the colours we know he used in the later stage of his career.[23] Alongside the more traditional pigments available to artists, such as earth colours, Prussian blue and emerald green, he did not hesitate to pick pigments that had only recently been introduced and that suited his work as a landscapist, such as viridian, cadmium yellow and strontium yellow. One of the conclusions based on the paint samples taken from the *Villerville* picture is that there is not much difference between his choice of pigments in the 1864 version and those used in the later reworkings. The subsequent sessions show different combinations of recurring, comparable groups of pigments, with one major difference: in the bottom layers these mixtures (relating to the original 1864 version of the painting) are dominated by light ochre and pinkish tones and they contain more lead white, whereas the layers applied in 1871–2, when large parts of the painting were reworked, tend towards dark ochre, greens and black tones.

The foreground of *Cliffs near Villerville* is characterised by underlying lighter series of paint layers on top of which thicker layers dominated by brown, greens and blacks were applied wet-in-wet with broader brushes and a palette knife. The rest of the painting received comparatively less attention during the reworking sessions; the opposite bank of the Seine, originally blueish green, was partially covered with a dark green layer, and the sky was given a new series of blue and warm grey passages in different shades. The village and the shrubs in front of it, as well as the woman and child, remained intact. One small but striking feature was also reworked: the bright top of the façade visible behind darker rooftops at the right half of the village was originally painted in beige, then covered with pink and finally highlighted with a thick Naples yellow (fig. 151), thereby drawing the observer's attention to the background, suggesting depth, and heightening the effect of juxtaposed shadows and highlights.

Parts of the foreground have cracked over time, exposing the bright colours of the underlying layers; in some cases, they have even risen to the surface. In one of the cross sections mentioned above (fig. 149), a different colour is present on top of the white ground: an opaque, bright red, probably vermilion, layer. Apart from one other sample with a yellow layer likewise on top of the ground, none of the other cross sections of the foreground shows the presence of such colours. Apparently, the artist chose to apply, at an early stage of the painting process and very locally, reds, oranges and yellows that were

subsequently completely covered. Traditionally, the first set up or blocking in of the main features of a composition would be done on top of the ground in diluted, dark colours. But it appears that Daubigny developed a preference for the use of bold colours in the first stage of painting.[24]

Paint Application: Liveliness and Impasto
In the nineteenth century, two different approaches to paint application can generally be distinguished – the 'painterly' and the 'graphic'. The latter is characterised by individual brushstrokes that remain more or less untouched: contours, hatchings, zigzag lines, dots and so on. A painterly approach on the other hand is concerned with larger zones of blended colours, either to function as flat areas or as volumes showing shadows, highlights and mid-tones juxtaposed. Until the advent of pointillist theory in the 1880s, artists rarely worked exclusively in either one or the other manner, the two approaches were often incorporated in the same painting. Daubigny's later landscapes were no exception in this regard.

As a great enthusiast for painting *en plein air*, Daubigny developed an effective technique for capturing different times of the day and types of weather in rapid succession. His smaller works in particular exhibit a hasty manner of painting typical of the artist who was attempting to record his initial impressions rapidly while the light was still good. Some of the looseness normally associated with painting outdoors was carried over to the larger works that he was unable to complete in front of the motif,

151
Photomicrograph of detail of Daubigny's
Cliffs near Villerville (fig. 131)

152
CHARLES FRANÇOIS DAUBIGNY
Ru de Valmondois, *c.* 1870–5 (detail of
top left corner)
Oil on canvas, 138.5 × 74.5 cm
The Mesdag Collection, The Hague

153
CHARLES FRANÇOIS DAUBIGNY
Sunset at Villerville, 1874
Detail of the top right corner of fig. 130 in raking
light, revealing how the paint, applied with a palette
knife, was given additional textures with a brush
while still wet.

154
CHARLES FRANÇOIS DAUBIGNY
Sunset, *c.* 1871 (detail of bottom right corner)
Oil on canvas, 103 × 203.5 cm
The Mesdag Collection, The Hague

or to their variants created within the confines of his studios in Paris and Auvers.

During the final stage of Daubigny's career he often applied colours swiftly, with wet-in-wet effects occurring in many places. However, most of the colours when still wet were not actually blended, but were left to dry after they had been applied. Highlights were added in quick succession, as were single brushstrokes with different colours picked up with the brush and smeared next to each other in one movement without proper mixing. Sky areas especially show such effects. Generally, these rapid strokes have a distinctly graphic effect, such as the zigzag line in *Banks of the Oise* (fig. 124) or the hatch-like brushstrokes used in sky areas and foreground, which bring to mind the experience Daubigny gained when creating his many etchings during the earlier part of his career.

Critical response to Daubigny's later, and freer, manner of painting landscapes was not always favourable. His relatively loose style engendered hostile reactions from some writers, whereas others favourably compared his brushwork to that of the English painter John Constable (1776–1837), who had been so admired in the earlier decades of the nineteenth century.[25] Contemporary comments on Daubigny's paintings made particular reference to the rich textured, impastoed layers of paint.[26] Such was his manner from the late 1860s onwards, that observers could no longer ignore the all-over free brushwork and application of generous amounts of paint. The latter especially was linked to the use of the palette knife. However, unlike Gustave Courbet's sophisticated and calculated use of this tool, which resulted in subtle shapes and passages of light and shadow, Daubigny did not shy away from smearing thicker unblended layers of colour in broad movements, like bold statements, and he often used brushes to rework areas applied with the palette knife or to create swiftly painted and unblended passages, adding to the texture and liveliness of the paint surface. Such effects can already be made out on a smaller scale in the sky of *Boats on the Thames* (fig. 155), painted *en plein air* during his 1866 visit to London.

From the early 1870s onwards the combination of different tools as well as unblended colours was also employed by Daubigny in a more obvious manner in the large-scale works, as can be seen in the foliage at the top of *Ru de Valmondois* (fig. 152), the sky area of *Sunset at Villerville* (fig. 153) and the foreground of *Sunset* (*c.* 1871). In the latter an unusual sequence of horizontal bands of blue, yellow and red opaque paints was applied with a palette knife. As if to diminish the startling, modern effect of these primary colours, transparent brown bands of paint were then brushed over them (fig. 154).

Conclusion

Towards the end of his career Daubigny stated he was not aware of having a working method and that he tried to paint as directly and as rapidly as possible what he saw or felt.[27] This is a remark by an artist who aimed to present himself as an experienced, independent

155
CHARLES FRANÇOIS DAUBIGNY
Boats on the Thames, c. 1866–7
Oil on canvas, 40.8 × 67 cm
The Mesdag Collection, The Hague

and above all non-academic modern painter. His contemporaries certainly agreed on this point when they discussed his works in their Salon reviews and writings on the current state of landscape painting.

Daubigny's later landscapes represent a break from conventional contemporary studio practice. Technical examination has revealed he started to experiment with supports in new formats, and that from the early 1870s onwards he had a tendency to apply not only paint layers but also grounds using a palette knife. Many of his later landscapes, especially the larger ones, show signs of reworking, addition and revision. In this Daubigny's approach to the painting process and to finishing his compositions became less straightforward and he moved away from the traditional, academic canon of *esquisse*, *ébauche* and *tableau fini*. Instead of aiming for smoother surfaces and a controlled balance between broader passages and carefully executed details, which remained the norm in academic landscape painting, the surfaces of Daubigny's late works show a bold use of both palette knife and brushes throughout.

In the paintings he made after his return from exile in London – sunsets off the Normandy coast, apple orchards, moonlit fields and panoramic views of the Oise and Seine rivers – Daubigny successfully managed to incorporate in his palette new colours that had only recently become available to artists, such as cadmium orange and yellow and cerulean blue. In his use of these bright, opaque colours, he not only showed a readiness to apply new materials, but also that he was alert to the new aesthetics in landscape painting offered by younger painters such as Camille Pissarro and Claude Monet.

156
CLAUDE MONET
Fishing Nets at Pourville, 1882
Oil on canvas, 60 × 81.5 cm
Gemeentemuseum, The Hague

Chronology

Lynne Ambrosini and Katie G. Benedict

1817 Charles François Daubigny is born in Paris, 54 rue Vieille du Temple. His father, Edme-François, is also a landscape painter.

1818–1826 Sickly as a child, Daubigny is sent to Valmondois, a village on the River Oise north of Paris. He spends several years there, cared for by his wet-nurse 'La Mère Bazot', and develops a lifelong affinity for nature.

1830 Birth of Camille Pissarro.

1832 To help support his family, the young Daubigny decorates jewellery boxes and clock faces. Birth of Edouard Manet.

1834 Daubigny works in Paris restoring paintings at the Louvre but often returns to Valmondois at weekends. His mother dies on 2 April. Birth of Edgar Degas.

1835 Daubigny enters the atelier of the academic painter Pierre-Asthasie-Théodore Sentiès. He continues his restoration work at Versailles to earn money for travel to Italy.

1836 Daubigny and fellow painter Henri Mignan leave for Italy on 20 February. After a stay in Rome, they paint in southern Italy.

1837 Returns from Italy and enters the competition for the Prix de Rome in historical landscape but does not win.

1838 Daubigny's first successful submission, the *View of Notre Dame and the Ile Saint Louis,* appears at the Salon. He works as a draughtsman and engraver.

1839 Daubigny travels to the Dauphiné, south-east France, in search of inspiration for his next Salon painting. Births of Paul Cézanne and Alfred Sisley.

1840 Exhibits *Saint Jerome in the Desert*, a historical landscape, and *View from the Oisans Valley* at the Salon. He enrols in the studio of Paul Delaroche so as to improve his chances in the 1841 Prix de Rome competition. Claude Monet is born in November.

1841 Daubigny is eliminated from the Prix de Rome competition after misunderstanding the rules; he gives up on the Prix. Births of Berthe Morisot, Armand Guillaumin, Pierre-Auguste Renoir and Frédéric Bazille.

1842 On 29 December Daubigny marries Marie-Sophie Garnier.

1843 Birth of Daubigny's daughter, Cécile. Throughout the decade, he continues to submit work regularly to the Salon. In the autumn, he works on his future Salon of 1844 painting outdoors in the Forest of Fontainebleau.

1846 Daubigny spends the summer in Valmondois. His son Charles, the future painter Karl Daubigny, is born there.

1848 The February Revolution marks the establishment of the French Republic. This liberalises the Salon; Daubigny is allowed to exhibit six paintings and wins a second-class medal. He also receives a state commission for an etching after Claude Lorrain's *The Watering Place*.

1849 By this date, Daubigny and Camille Corot have begun a life-long friendship.

1852 Both of Daubigny's Salon submissions, *The Harvest* and *View from the Banks of the Seine at Bezons* are purchased by the French government. Art critics pay attention. In *Le Moniteur Universel*, Daubigny's work is likened unfavourably to a sketch (*ébauche*) for the first time. Daubigny and Corot travel together to Crémieu and Optevoz in France and Dardagny in Switzerland.

1853 Birth of a second son, Bernard. Daubigny's Salon submission *The Pond at Gylieu* is purchased by Emperor Napoleon III. Birth of Vincent van Gogh.

1854 Daubigny travels throughout France, notably discovering the fishing village of Villerville in Normandy.

1855 Daubigny spends the summer in Normandy and Brittany. His *Sluice in the Valley of Optevoz* wins a third-class medal at the Paris Exposition Universelle and is purchased by the French government. He is called a master of realism.

1857 Daubigny launches his studio boat, the *Botin*, on the River Seine. His painting, *Spring*, of an orchard in blossom, is widely acclaimed as a highly original new form of subject matter.

1859 Daubigny is made a Chevalier de la Légion d'Honneur. He submits five paintings to the Salon including *Banks of the Oise*, purchased by the photographer Nadar, and wins a first-class medal. Collectors seek out his work. Monet admires Daubigny's Salon submissions, while Pissarro makes his debut at the Salon.

1860 Daubigny buys land in Auvers-sur-Oise and builds a house and studio there by 1862. Henceforth he lives both in Paris and Auvers. He visits Gustave Courbet in Ornans in November. Monet receives a small sketch by Daubigny for *The Grape Harvest at Twilight* as a gift from his aunt.

1861 Daubigny visits Courbet again in spring. The critic Théophile Gautier blames Daubigny for showing only 'first impressions' and 'neglecting details' in his Salon paintings: Daubigny makes the etchings that will become *Le Voyage en bateau*, published in 1862. On one, he inscribes the word 'réalisme'.

1863 In Auvers, Daubigny hosts Morisot and her family for a meal. He makes trips down the Seine and Oise in the *Botin* and also travels to Villerville, by now the site of regular summer trips with his family.

1864 Morisot and Renoir exhibit paintings at the Salon. Daubigny shows his *Cliffs near Villerville*, a large canvas that he worked on outdoors the previous autumn. Monet's paintings of the Pointe de la Hève at Sainte-Adresse show a strong awareness of Daubigny.

1865 Daubigny travels to London in July where he meets James Abbott McNeill Whistler and has lunch at his house. Monet and Edgar Degas make their Salon debuts.

1866 Daubigny is elected to the Salon jury, where he vehemently defends the work of Cézanne, Pissarro and Renoir. By this date, he has met Monet in Normandy near Honfleur. He visits London again.

1867 Bazille circulates a petition to hold a second Salon des Refusés. It is signed by Monet, Manet, Sisley, Pissarro, Renoir and Daubigny.

1868 Daubigny's paintings are increasingly bold and loose in style. Odilon Redon calls him 'the painter of a moment, of an impression'. Daubigny shows work in an exhibition in Le Havre with Courbet, Manet and Monet. Daubigny is re-elected to the Salon jury and successfully campaigns to admit paintings by Pissarro, Monet, Bazille, Degas, Renoir, Sisley and Morisot.

1870 Daubigny resigns from the Salon jury when a painting by Monet is rejected. Franco-Prussian War declared in July. Daubigny and his family, then in Villerville, seek refuge in London in October. One of Daubigny's dealers, Paul Durand-Ruel, opens a gallery there. Daubigny introduces Monet and Pissarro, who have also relocated to London, to Durand-Ruel.

1871 The International Exhibition of 1871 opens in London in May; Daubigny exhibits nine paintings. Later, the Daubigny family, including newborn granddaughter Charlotte, returns to France. Daubigny and his son Karl travel to the Netherlands in the autumn.

1872 Daubigny continues his habit of frequent painting trips in the *Botin* on the Oise and other rivers. He also takes the waters at Cauterets to improve his health; in addition to gout, he has developed asthma and bronchitis. Pissarro settles in Pontoise, near Daubigny's home, and Cézanne joins him there the following year. Monet buys and launches his own studio boat at Argenteuil. Charles Sedelmeyer commissions *Moonrise* from Daubigny at the unprecedented price of 20,000 francs.

1873 Daubigny and Cézanne meet while painting outside near Auvers. Daubigny's *Moonrise* from the 1868 Salon is refined and exhibited at Vienna's International Exposition to great acclaim. Daubigny is made an Officier de la Légion d'Honneur. He buys Monet's *A Zaan in Saardam [Holland]* from Durand-Ruel.

1874 Monet exhibits *Impression: Sunrise* at the first exhibition of the group of artists later known as the Impressionists. The term 'Impressionism' is officially coined by critic Louis Leroy. Encouraged by the work of the younger painters, Daubigny paints very freely and with more vivid colours.

1875 Corot dies in February. Daubigny is in poor health himself. Van Gogh sees paintings by Daubigny in Goupil's London gallery and admires them greatly.

1876 Asthma interrupts Daubigny's plans to travel on the *Botin*, so he paints at Auvers instead. He goes to Dieppe, Honfleur and Villerville later that year. He paints many sunsets and nocturnes.

1877 At the 1877 Salon, Daubigny exhibits *Dieppe* and *Moonrise*. That summer, he takes his final trip on the studio boat.

1878 Daubigny works on his last canvas, *Moonrise at Auvers*. Emile Zola praises it: 'It is the soul of nature that speaks to you.' Daubigny dies in Paris on 19 February. Two paintings are exhibited at the Salon, and the Paris Exposition Universelle includes a small retrospective of his more recent works. His studio and its contents are sold in May. Daubigny is buried in the family crypt at the cemetery of Père Lachaise in Paris, near to Corot's grave. In July, Durand-Ruel pays homage to Daubigny and other recently deceased landscape painters by organising a show of their work at his gallery; it features eighteen paintings by Daubigny. Monet's paintings of the Seine at Vétheuil and nearby Lavacourt reflect a renewed interest in the older artist.

1880 Van Gogh decides to become an artist. In his letters, he repeatedly speaks of the greatness of Daubigny, Jean-François Millet and Théodore Rousseau, and of their deep appreciation of nature. Monet's *The Seine at Lavacourt*, strongly influenced by Daubigny, is accepted at the Salon.

1886 Van Gogh moves to Paris, where his brother Theo works for the art dealers Boussod, Valadon & Cie (previously Goupil & Cie). There he meets many progressive painters and adopts the bright palette of Impressionism.

1888 Van Gogh moves to Arles, in Provence, southern France. Towards the end of the year, coinciding with a visit from Paul Gauguin, he has a mental crisis and breakdown.

1889 In May Van Gogh admits himself to the Saint-Paul asylum at Saint-Rémy.

1890 In order to be under the care of Dr Gachet, who lives in Auvers, Van Gogh moves to the village famed as Daubigny's home. He visits Daubigny's widow and paints her garden in homage to the older painter whom he admired. Unable to fight off his illness and depression, Van Gogh takes his own life in July.

Notes

PREFACE
Lynne Ambrosini
pp. 12–13

1. As misconceptions about Daubigny abound, this seems an appropriate opportunity to put the record straight. Since the 1890s, writers have treated him in tandem with 'the Barbizon School' of artists (see n. 2 below), which has led to errors. Statements that Daubigny painted primarily in the Forest of Fontainebleau; worked side by side with Théodore Rousseau, Jean-François Millet, or Narcisse Diaz de la Peña; lived in the village of Barbizon for long periods or had a house there are, to the best of our knowledge, untrue. He visited the Forest on three documented occasions between 1843 and 1861. He also crossed or passed by the Forest on his way to Italy in 1836 at the age of nineteen (Georgel 2007, p. 40 and p. 75 n. 13). We know that he stayed in Barbizon in October 1843 (Moreau-Nélaton 1925, pp. 37–8). He was in Marlotte, another nearby village, sometime in the summer of 1857 (Fidell-Beaufort and Bailly-Herzberg 1975, p. 490). He stayed at the Auberge Ganne in Barbizon once after 1861 (Billy 2002, p. 78). Out of the approximately 1,240 paintings listed in Hellebranth's catalogue raisonné, only seven are believed to represent Barbizon or the Fontainebleau forest. In short, it appears that Daubigny rarely painted there.
   A second misapprehension is that Daubigny painted river views exclusively. Of the 1,240 pictures that Hellebranth catalogued, less than half (560) depict rivers. Daubigny also portrayed meadows, farmhouses, ponds, coasts, ports, boats, mountains, orchards and woodland scenes. This exhibition demonstrates some of his range and variety. Equally erroneous is a third claim that Daubigny devoted himself exclusively to the River Oise. Some 280 of the paintings in Hellebranth do depict the Oise, but another 130 render sites on the Seine. Daubigny first launched his famous studio boat on the Seine, not the Oise (as is often said). He also visited and depicted the Marne, Loire, Loing, Yonne, Vilaine, Erdre, Cousin and other rivers. Beyond the Ile de France, he portrayed landscapes in Burgundy, the Dauphiné, Normandy, Brittany, Bordeaux, the Pyrenees, England and Holland.
   Finally, although Daubigny's defence of younger painters while serving on the Salon jury in 1866, 1868 and 1870 was valuable, it would be mistaken to consider it his primary legacy. The authors of this book argue that Daubigny's artistic practice itself mattered even more in shaping future art. His interactions with younger painters were complex and interesting. Between about 1859 and 1869, his art directly influenced the next generation, while they in turn affected his style in the 1870s. The story of Van Gogh's interest in Daubigny forms a remarkable epilogue.
2. Some survey exhibitions on 'Barbizon' landscape have included works by Daubigny. While important, these have afforded little opportunity to study his art in depth. See Herbert 1962; Busch 1980; Sillevis and Kraan 1985; Champa 1991; Tinterow and Loyrette 1994; Heilmann *et al.* 1996; and Pomarède and Wallens 2002. Recent exhibitions focused on the Forest of Fontainebleau (Georgel 2007 and Jones *et al.* 2008), have not included Daubigny. It should be noted that, although David Croal Thomson coined the term 'Barbizon' (Thomson 1890) to denote painters who worked in the Forest of Fontainebleau or the nearby village of Barbizon, there was no formal group by this name and the term was not used during the artists' lifetimes.

'LEADER OF THE SCHOOL OF THE IMPRESSION': DAUBIGNY AND HIS LEGACY
Lynne Ambrosini
pp. 15–43

1. Born in 1817, Daubigny was about the same age as Courbet, J. Jongkind and H.J. Harpignies, all born in 1819.
2. Castagnary 1892, vol. 2, p. 353. All translations from the French are by the author.
3. Léon Lagrange 1865, in Daguet 1971, p. 45. Cited by kind permission of the author.
4. Conisbee *et al.* 1996, pp. 268–9, no. 125.
5. Boime 1970, pp. 187–90. On Daubigny's graphic work, see Fidell 1974.
6. See the amusing letter of 4 August 1839 in Fidell-Beaufort and Bailly-Herzberg 1975, p. 236.
7. On this painting and the next, see Ambrosini 2002, pp. 396–400.
8. See the sketch of the artist 'loaded like a pack-mule'; letter, Moreau-Nélaton 1925, pp. 3–38 and fig. 20.
9. Marlais *et al.* 2004; and Marlais 2008.
10. Ambrosini 2002, pp. 398–400.
11. In particular, Corot's *Souvenir of Volterra*, Salon of 1838, National Gallery of Art, Washington DC.
12. Fidell-Beaufort and Bailly-Herzberg 1975, Letter VII, p. 256. The area was popular with artists; for example, Harpignies, J.A. Achard and the Lyonnais painter Paul Flandrin worked there in July 1847; Clarke 1986, p. 52.
13. Ambrosini 2002, p. 409 n. 41. Daubigny and Corot remained close friends for life.
14. A study on panel preceded the larger painting; Hellebranth 1976, p. 323, no. 982.
15. Letter, 23 August 1852, in Fidell-Beaufort and Bailly-Herzberg 1975, p. 257.
16. An oil on panel study for this painting (29 × 53 cm) sold at Sotheby's, New York, 4 May 1979, lot 205.
17. Guégan *et al.* 1992, p. 90. Louis Clément de Ris concurred (Clément de Ris 1852, p. 99).
18. Burmester and Denk 1999, pp. 303–8.
19. Tillot 1852, no. 6011.
20. Du Camp 1852, p. 143. Five other reviewers took positions somewhere between the two poles. For this project, periodicals across the political spectrum and ranging from intellectual to popular publications have been consulted.
21. Henriet 1857, p. 196. The Cincinnati picture is the Salon canvas; its reverse bears a label from the Rainbeaux family. Firmin Rainbeaux was the personal agent to Louis Napoleon Bonaparte and bought the painting for display at the Palace of Saint-Cloud; object file, Cincinnati Art Museum.
22. Clément de Ris 1853, p. 147.
23. Bertall 1853, no. 95, p. 2.
24. Some, though, were quick to distinguish it from the 'ugly' realism of Courbet; Mouriez 1853, p. 2. On Daubigny's realism, see also Viel-Castel 1853, p. 609, and earlier still, Du Pays 1852, pp. 427–8.
25. Gautier 1853, pp. 1–2.
26. The drawing 'Marée basse sur une côte' bears a note '3 h' (3 o'clock); Musée d'Orsay, Département des Arts Graphiques, RF 9119 recto.
27. Millette 2004, and personal communication on 26 November 2007 and 9 January 2008.
28. This can be deduced from the unfinished lower right side. It was probably unfinished because it was a gift to a friend and fellow artist, Adolphe Appian; it is inscribed: 'Don de Daubigny à Appian, 1856.'
29. Known as *vert émeraude* in France, viridian is a cool, dark transparent green. Daubigny employed it *before* its commercial release in 1862; (this is a correction to Ambrosini 2002, p. 404). It was identified in a painting dated 1859; Emily Gore, Scientific Department, National Gallery, London, April 2000. That unpublished information was not available to me in 2002. I also learned late in 2002 about a technical article in German that revealed viridian was available from its inventor as early as the 1830s through one supplier in Paris; Burmester and Denk 1999, p. 298.
30. Burmester and Denk 1999, p. 303. In the 1850s, Daubigny began to use cobalt blue and Schweinfurt green; ibid., p. 308.
31. For more picturesque early views of the coast, see Herbert 1994, pp. 18, 34 and 64–7, and House *et al.* 2007, pp. 21–5.
32. Letter, 23 June 1854, in Moreau-Nélaton 1925, p. 62.
33. He painted double-width formats from about 1855 until his death. See Hellebranth 1976.
34. Joseph Ruzicka, unpublished collection catalogue, 28 December 1990, p. 2, Curatorial file, Department of European Art, Brooklyn Museum. Daubigny is known to have visited Mantes with Corot sometime in the 1850s.
35. On Pissarro, see Brettell 1990, pp. 87–8; Rothkopf and Lloyd 2007, pp. 164–7, entry by Gülru Çakmak.
36. Henriet 1875, p. 189.
37. Henriet 1876, pp. 96–7.
38. Daubigny included smokestacks in *Vue aux environs de Paris, près d'Argenteuil*, Musée des Beaux-Arts, Limoges, and in *Rouen*, 61 × 91 cm, Parke-Bernet sale catalogue, New York, 6 April 1960, lot 58.
39. In 1854 he was dismayed to find trees razed near Avallon; Fidell-Beaufort and Bailly-Herzberg 1975, p. 259. On his participation in an environmental action in 1873, see Georgel 2007, p. 165.
40. Gautier 1857, p. 114. Corot's student Armand Gautier [no relation] reported on public response to the Salon: 'The talk is only of Daubigny and Corot.' Monneret 1994, p. 11.
41. Castagnary 1892, vol. 1, p. 22. Du Pays 1857, p. 203; see also Tardieu 1857a and 1857b. Both a preliminary drawing and an oil *esquisse* are known; Moreau-Nélaton 1925, p. 132, and Hellebranth 1976, no. 956.
42. Letter, 1881, Musée d'Orsay, Aut.351, AR13, pp. 85–7.
43. Green 1990, pp. 67–116. See also Gautier 1853, pp. 1–2.
44. Letter to La Rochenoire, 27 July 1874, in Michel 1904, p. 562.
45. Lacambre 1974, p. 60, no. 63. It was exhibited also at the Expositions Universelles of 1867 and 1878 in Paris.
46. Respectively, at the Salons of 1859, 1867, 1868, 1869 and 1870, he showed *Les champs au Printemps*; *Printemps, soleil couché*; *Printemps*; *Un Verger*; and *Un sentier, fin du mois de Mai*. *Le verger* of 1868 is illustrated in Moreau-Nélaton 1925, between pp. 98 and 99, fig. 87. Hellebranth 1976, pp. 313–19. On Van Gogh's admiration for Daubigny's 1857 *Spring*, see the essay by Nienke Bakker in this volume.
47. Among the smaller works were an *Apple Trees in Blossom* of 1860–2 (Israel Museum, Jerusalem); a larger canvas called *May* of 1862 (G. Petit, Paris, Louis Sarlin sale, 2 March 1918, lot 22); a *Road of the Apple Trees* commissioned by the dealer Hector Brame in 1868 (according to Daubigny's Account Books [Raskin-Daubigny], 1856–77, p. 42. This source is a facsimile compilation of several account books in one binder with numbered pages, given to the author in 2005 by Daniel Raskin-Daubigny, a now-deceased descendant of the artist. However, some lost pages from the original account books are missing.) Other orchard paintings included: *Crabapple Blossoms* of 1868 and an *Apple Tree in Bloom* of 1869 (Anderson Galleries, New York, 2 August 1931, lot 49 and p. 67); a flowering *Orchard* of 1871 (Sotheby's, New York, 30 March 1966, *Le Verger*, lot 47); a replica of that in 1872 (Parke-Bernet Galleries, New York, 26

May 1943); and other examples in Hellebranth 1976, nos 970–81.

48 The Monet (Union League Club, Chicago); illustrated in Wildenstein 1996, vol. 2, p. 92, no. 201.

49 At the Impressionist exhibition of 1874, Castagnary admired this work but lamented Pissarro's 'deplorable liking for market garden land'; Berson 1996, p. 16.

50 Paid 18 May 1857; Musée d'Orsay, Documentation, fiche oeuvre no. 117539. Daubigny's paintings at this time typically cost between 150 and 500 francs but he received 1,000 francs for a replica of the *Pond of Gylieu* in 1856; Account Books (Raskin-Daubigny), p. 8.

51 On Daubigny's poverty and frugality, see Rousseau 1857, p. 3.

52 Michael Clarke's essay in this volume explores the use of studio boats by Daubigny and Monet. See also Grad 1977.

53 On the site, see Laran and Crémieux 1912, p. 74, and Walter 1988, p. 31.

54 Charlotte Seifen Ameringer, Paintings Conservator, San Francisco Fine Arts Museums, 15 August 2002. On the brilliance of Daubigny's colourism, see Roy 1999, pp. 337–41.

55 Henriet 1857, p. 197.

56 Hellebranth 1976, nos 592, 716, 721–3.

57 Daubigny visited Courbet in Ornans in November 1860 and April 1861; Chu 1992, pp. 183 and 195. In a paper for the College Art Association, I explored their relationship: '"The Landscape Artists are Dead in the Water": Gustave Courbet and C.F. Daubigny', Los Angeles, 25 February 2009. Courbet's earlier sea pictures included beaches.

58 The photographer Félix Nadar purchased the painting and sold it to the Société des Amis des Arts of Bordeaux in 1863; object file, Musée des Beaux-Arts, Bordeaux. On Nadar's cartoon, see Tinterow and Loyrette 1994, p. 365.

59 Perrin 1859, p. 654. Compare to Alexandre Dumas: 'Un des grands succès de cette année, succès incontesté et incontestable, est à DAUBIGNY … Les paysages de Daubigny sont superbes et d'une grande vérité.' Dumas 1859, p. 87.

60 Castagnary 1892, vol. 2, pp. 71, 77. He compared Daubigny to the novelist Georges Sand.

61 Perrier 1859, p. 320. Eleven of the nineteen Salon reviewers that I read considered Daubigny a realist, though two of the eleven substituted the term 'naturalist' for realist.

62 Zola (1878); Fernandez 1997, p. 171.

63 Baudelaire 1968, 'Salon de 1959', p. 105.

64 Perrin 1859, p. 654.

65 See Shiff 1984, pp. 21–6, on this duality.

66 Astruc 1859, pp. 303–4.

67 He wrote of Auvers: 'It's very beautiful right down to Pontoise and has just given me the idea of undertaking the [river] descent and making studies.' Letter, 1860, in Moreau-Nélaton 1925, pp. 78–9.

68 Letter, 1860, Musée d'Orsay, Aut.354, AR14, pp. 3–4.

69 *Landscape with Field Workers*, oil on panel, 17.2 × 32.4 cm; New York, Christie's, 23 May 1991, lot 239; Hellebranth 1996, no. 215. *La Rentrée des foins*, about 1860 (atelier sale, 1878), oil on panel, 19 × 33 cm, Hellbranth 1976, no. 985. He also depicted the potato harvest, Trouville, 1861–2. Hellebranth 1976, nos 667–9. Pissarro's open-air farm studies of 1836–62 are very close to Daubigny's. Pissarro and Durand-Ruel Snollaerts 2005, vol. 2, nos 31, 34, 35, 38, 39, 57.

70 *La Machine à battre le blé*, 1860, illustrated Delteil 1921, no. 94.

71 Yriarte 1868, p. 403; Brettell 1990, pp. 58–61, on Pissarro.

72 Fidell-Beaufort and Bailly-Herzberg 1975, p. 47 n. 44 and p. 41 n. 29. Théodore Duret, Manet's friend and patron, wrote about Daubigny's river views: 'Vous avez un tableau qui, en quelques pieds carrés, vous permet, au milieu de la vie artificielle et murée des villes, de retrouver la nature et de jouir alors, comme en sa présence, de la sensation délicieuse de calme et de fraîcheur que son aspect fait naître.' Duret 1867, p. 37.

73 Dupâquier 1985–6, pp. 1–2. The Impressionists also pictured pre-modern agriculture; Brettell 1990, pp. 175–82.

74 *Le chemin de la plaine à Auvers*, 1843, private collection, France; a moonlit view in Hellebranth 1976, no. 139; a painting dated 1869; Hellebranth 1996, no. 74; a nocturnal view in Hellebranth 1976, no. 152; finally, the larger *Church at Auvers, Twilight*, Dixon Gallery and Gardens, Memphis, Tennessee.

75 Letter, 30 September 1872, Musée d'Orsay, Aut.367b, AR14, p. 17.

76 Corot visited often. Daumier settled nearby in 1865; Fidell-Beaufort and Bailly-Herzberg 1975, pp. 57, 68. On Pissarro, Berthe Morisot and Paul Cézanne in Auvers, see the essay by Frances Fowle in this volume.

77 Du Camp 1863, p. 916; Cantrel 1863, p. 199.

78 I see no reason to interpret this as a parody of realism, as did House 1986, p. 193. Given Daubigny's painstakingly observed works of the 1850s, there is every reason to believe that he endorsed Courbet's and Champfleury's *réalisme*. He shared their left-wing politics: he participated in a Fourierist 'phalanstery' in Paris in 1838; hummed songs by Béranger in 1839 (Fidell-Beaufort and Bailly-Herzberg 1975, p. 240); mentioned an intention to read a brochure by Proudhon in a letter in 1852 (Price 1967, p. 100); made sympathetic references to Barbès and Pierre Dupont, including referring to a Dupont song about famine and the common people, 'Le Chant du pain' (1847) (Fidell-Beaufort and Bailly-Herzberg 1975, p. 259); and tried to help a friend who was a Communard in 1871 (letter, 16 June 1871, Musée d'Orsay, Aut.347, AR13, pp. 78–9). When Castagnary proposed that they circulate an appeal for leniency for Courbet in 1873; Daubigny replied sadly: 'We would collect only three signatures: mine, Daumier's and Corot's; not one more.' Mack 1951, pp. 298–9 and p. 390 n. 10.

79 Nochlin 1966, a text of 1861.

80 Miquel 1994, pp. 178 and 184; Meignen 1996, p. 96.

81 The painting is inscribed 'Inondation de 1876 à Billancourt', but the date appears to be an error. Flooding along the Seine and Loire occurred in September 1866; Belgrand and Lemoine 1866, pp. 162–7. There were floods on the Seine in 1876, too, but they occurred between February and April; Cheysson and Camère 1877, p. 49. The painting shows autumn foliage, so it must represent the flood of 1866. Daubigny often dated works when selling them; Hellebranth 1976, p. ix. Daubigny may have sold the incomplete painting in 1876, and may (accidentally or not) have written a 7 instead of a 6. The style of the painting and its elaborate preparatory drawing also suggest the earlier date.

82 Henriet 1875, p. 45. Ground information is based on study of some sixty-seven conservation examinations and treatment reports on Daubigny's paintings kindly communicated by American and European museums. By varying the ground colour, Daubigny could set a chromatic key for his paintings.

83 Salon of 1867; Johnston 1982, no. 67. Hellebranth 1976 identifies two views of Andrésy as the Salon picture, but the Walters painting is the correct one; nos 49, 50.

84 *Itinéraire des Bateaux à Vapeur de Paris au Havre*, Paris, n.d., pp. 48 and 51. Some forty different guides were published; Joubert *et al*. 1994, p. 245. Also Barron 1889, p. 318.

85 Daubigny painted Vétheuil at least twice, in about 1872 and 1876; atelier sale catalogue, 1878, p. 39, no. 268, and p. 56, no. 401. He also painted Lavacourt, across the Seine, in about 1873 and 1877; ibid, p. 44, no. 305, and p. 61, no. 437. He sold a painting of Giverny to a Mr Estienne on 17 May 1858, Account Books (Raskin-Daubigny), p. 22. Monet settled in Vétheuil in 1878, and painted it and Lavacourt until about 1881.

86 Romantic artists who depicted Seine sites included J.M.W. Turner, J. Gendall and R.P. Bonington.

87 A hundred freight steamboats already circulated between Paris and Rouen in the 1840s. Miquel 1994, pp. 159, 189, 199.

88 Joubert *et al.* 1994, p. 280.

89 Letter, 28 October 1857, Musée d'Orsay, Aut.367b, AR13, pp. 69–70.

90 *Le Botin passant au large des bateaux*, ink on paper, Musée d'Orsay, Département des Arts Graphiques, RF 5330 recto.

91 *Le Passage des bateaux à vapeur*, ink on paper, Musée d'Orsay, Département des Arts Graphiques, RF 5329 recto.

92 Similarly, Monet excluded motorised barges from his paintings of the Seine; Brettell 1996, p. 126.

93 A larger, more finished version is in the Musée d'Orsay, s.d. 1865 (RF 1806); Lemoine 1976, p. 96.

94 Or the holes may have been pierced earlier, in order to attach the panel to a portable easel. Daubigny's studio contained a 'prodigieuse multitude d'esquisses, rapportées de ses voyages, qui s'entassent dans les coins, s'empilent sur les meubles, ou s'étalent tout autour de l'atelier'; Henriet 1857, p. 198. A later visitor described the studio as 'tout tapissé de petites études', Claretie 1882–4, vol. 1, p. 265.

95 Jean-Aubry and Schmit 1968, pp. 70–2.

96 Champa 1985 [facsimile of 1973 ed.], pp. 59–60; Herbert 1988, pp. 204–5; Brenneman and Champa 1999, p. 59.

97 See Bomford *et al*. 1999, pp. 120–1.

98 See above, n. 75.

99 Castagnary 1892, vol. 1, p. 77. Another acquaintance of Daubigny said his work was founded on the principle 'que l'allure d'un tableau doit refléter la sensation éprouvée.' Wolff 1886, pp. 150–1.

100 Henriet 1875, pp. 44–5. Asked about his method, Daubigny replied, 'I try to paint as directly and as rapidly as possible what I see and feel'. Tryon 1896, pp. 163, 161.

101 1874, reprinted in Berson 1996, vol. 1, p. 17.

102 Richard Shiff has discussed a similar ambiguity in Cézanne's use of the word 'sensation'; Shiff 2012, p. 35.

103 The Salons were held in the spring. On the October trip, see Fidell-Beaufort and Bailly-Herzberg 1975, p. 54.

104 Henriet 1875, p. 43. Henriet used the word *ébauche*, which was a full-scale colour preparation.

105 Examples of colour preparations on canvases from the 1870s also survive; see *Chateau Gaillard*, c. 1873 (Museum of Fine Arts, Boston); Roy 1999, p. 334. Daubigny painted or began a medium-size work outdoors, before a windmill in Holland, in 1871; it is visible in an illustrated letter reproduced in Henriet 1881, p. 77.

106 Yriarte 1868, p. 403.

107 Henriet 1875, p. 43. We also know that Daubigny later reworked this painting in the studio; see the essay by René Boitelle in this volume. On Monet's studio work, for example, see Clarke 2003, p. 131.

108 For more on the topic, see the essay in this volume on Daubigny's market. See also Wolff 1886, pp. 145–51.

109 Henriet 1875, p. 43. Henriet makes the story colourful by indicating the risks that an outdoor painter faced, such as children's pranks and cows from the nearby pastures, but does not state that Daubigny's canvas actually suffered such incidents. This is figurative writing in the best nineteenth-century tradition.

110 On Monet's series, see Tucker 1989, Chapters 4–8.

111 Castagnary 1892, vol. 2, p. 193.
112 De Sault 1864, p. 1.
113 'Nous n'y voyons que des ébauches, des études largement brossées, d'une touche strapassée.' Du Pays 1864, p. 39. The word 'strapassé', no longer in use, came from Italian (strapazzato) and meant 'painted in a coarse, careless headlong manner as if the object of the painter had been to get done'; Osborn and Bouvier 1856, p. 390.
114 'M. Daubigny a parfaitement compris que … si l'on devait retrouver le grand style, on ne le retrouverait que par la vigueur des ses propres impressions …'; Lafenestre 1864, p. 362.
115 La Fizelière 1864, pp. 1–2.
116 Lagrange 1864, pp. 10, 11.
117 Daguet 1971, p. 45. Cited by permission of the author.
118 He was the first to paint in Concarneau, Penmarc'h and Kérity; Moreau-Nélaton 1925, pp. 96–7. Delouche 1977, pp. 268–73.
119 James Horns, Paintings Conservator, Minneapolis, examined 20 March 1996; Daubigny applied fluid impastos wet-into-wet without reworking. He laid in a priming layer with a wide knife, using slashing, crisscross marks that do not correspond to the composition; these show up in raking light. Similar diagonal edge marks underlie his Beach at Villerville at Sunset; Mark Lewis, Chrysler Museum of Art, 29 June 2012. See the essay by René Boitelle in this volume.
120 Probably the Taliferme (84 × 145 cm) in Daubigny's posthumous sale catalogue, p. 25, no. 164, with a proposed date of 1865 there, but more likely this dates from the 1867 trip. Writing that year, Daubigny praised the beauty of Brittany, 'bordée de rochers noirs au bord de la mer'; Moreau-Nélaton 1925, p. 97.
121 However, this unsigned painting may be unfinished; it remained in the artist's studio upon his death.
122 Castagnary 1892, p. 272. Castagnary (b. 1830) was apparently unaware of Daubigny's earlier usage. The error has been much repeated. Daubigny's palette knife use in finished pictures was also noted in Henriet 1857, p. 196. See the essay by René Boitelle in this volume.
123 See Rózsa-Kaposy 1979, p. 171.
124 Chesneau 1868, p. 1. Cham [pseudonym of Amédée de Noé (1819–1879)] presented it as a metallic disc shining on a metal landscape, with the caption, Paysage d'Alsace, effet de nuit, 'tableaux de ce qui brillent le plus en Alsace. Important réserve metallique'. In another cartoon, he showed the two peasants in the foreground of Daubigny's picture fleeing in disgust from an overripe cheese in the sky: 'Paysans incommodés par un fromage fort faisant l'intérim pour la lune.' Cham 1868. Bertall showed the moon as a coin. Illustrated in Chabanne 1990, pp. 34–6. André Gill caricatured Daubigny's moon as a huge clock with the caption, Effet de lune – de Genève, huit trous en rubis, garantie 10 ans, par M. Daubigny, Gill 1868. See the mention of the brouhaha: 'cette lune jaune à laquelle les plaisants s'acharnent.' Castagnary 1892, vol. 2, p. 271.
125 Lemaire (1868) 1986, p. 229; Grangedor 1868, p. 27.
126 Daubigny listed the names of James Whistler, Alphonse Legros, Valentine Prinsep, Seymour Haden, Frederic Leighton, Barbara Bodichon and Lawrence Alma-Tadema, along with some dealers and suppliers; Account Books (Raskin-Daubigny), pp. 86–93. On Daubigny, Monet and Pissarro in London, see the essay by Maite van Dijk in this volume.
127 Daubigny created it rapidly in one session with no later changes, thus probably en plein air. David Marquis, Upper Midwest Conservation Association, 17 September 1990. For more detail, see Ambrosini 2002, pp. 406–8.
128 The Toledo Museum of Art recently acquired another of Daubigny's sweeping views of the fields above Auvers, Auvers, Landscape with Plough, c. 1877, 46.5 × 81.5 cm, which is probably no. 433 in Daubigny's 1878 estate sale, 'Le Blés (Printemps)'. It is a progressive, broadly painted canvas with vivid green fields under a grey-white sky. It is included in this exhibition at the Taft venue only.

129 The sky may have been overcleaned, perhaps in its 1943 conservation during which 'discolored varnishes were removed'. Johnston 1982, p. 76, no. 68. In paintings in which Daubigny mixed pigments with resinous materials, varnish cannot be safely removed; tinted glazes and pigment might come off with it. Keith and White 2002, pp. 4–8.
130 For more compositions of this type, see Hellebranth 1976, nos 592, 630, 646–8, 651, 721, 722, 730.
131 Anderberg 2011, p. 96.
132 In this, it contrasts with some contemporary, richly detailed coastal images. For example, in 1874, Eugène Boudin painted groups of elegant vacationers on the beach in Beach Scene in Trouville, c. 1874, Yale University Art Gallery (http://artgallery.yale.edu/collections/objects/beach-scene-trouville), while Monet rendered the Port of Le Havre in 1874 with ships, pedestrians, docks and buildings (http://www.philamuseum.org/collections/permanent/58675.html?mulR=2096128159|1).
133 Harrison 1991, p. 129. There were likely two versions of this painting; one sold in Daubigny's posthumous atelier sale of 1878 (p. 39, no. 265), as 'Retour de pêche (Villerville)'. The dealer Karl Sedelmeyer commissioned 'une répétition … de la plage' from Daubigny for 8,000 francs; Account Book (Musée d'Orsay), Aut.367b, AR16, pp. 22–3, with drawing. It was exhibited at the Exposition Universelle in Vienna; Sedelmeyer 1873, p. 102, no. 171.
134 See Brettell and Shaefer 1984, pp. 41–9, Herbert, 1994; and Green 1990, pp. 93 and 109. Also Baranowski and Furlough 2001, pp. 8–13.
135 Janin 1844, for example, contains many illustrations by Daubigny.
136 Letter of 23 June 1854, in Fidell-Beaufort and Bailly-Herzberg 1975, p. 257.
137 Letter, 1854, Musée d'Orsay, Aut.367b, AR13, p. 63.
138 '… formerly only inhabited by fisherman, and visited by artists, but of later years [Villerville] has begun to build villas, and has now a regular bathing establishment.' Macquoid 1875, p. 320. E.J. Dantan painted the later boardwalk and villas atop its cliffs in Villerville-sur-Mer, 1881, oil on panel; Talabardon and Gautier 2007, no. 24.
139 Grand salon carré; Anon. 1873, p. 2. Some 2,142 works were on view.
140 Merson 1873, p. 39. He was an academic artist.
141 De Hauranne 1873, p. 862; also Mantz 1873, p. 2.
142 Stop 1873, p. 5.
143 Castagnary 1892, vol. 2, pp. 59–60. Jules Claretie also considered the painting 'un prodige de couleur et de force … cette immensité de la mer labourée de couleur, tout cela est superbe'. Claretie 1882–4, vol. 1, p. 284.
144 See the reproductive etching by Théophile Chauvel, 1876; Delteil 1900, pp. 14, 49–50, 81. The painting should probably be called Spring, the engraving's title, as Chauvel generally preserved painters' original titles.
145 Slightly north-east of Auvers, Valmondois is an easy walk from it. Rû, in dialect, means 'brook'. Daubigny's close friend, the sculptor Geoffroy-Dechaume, with whom he spent time in Valmondois as a youth, owned the earliest known depiction of the motif, about 1835, with flowering spring trees; Hellebranth 1976, no. 216. See also Hellebranth 1976, nos 182, 183, 190, 195, 196, 205, 209, 212, 218 and 220, and Hellebranth 1996, no. 90.
146 Daubigny tried moonlit scenes in etchings in 1845 and again in the early 1860s; Fidell 1974, p. 57. At the 1859 Salon, he showed La rentrée du berger, effect de lune; in 1861, a Lever de lune and Parc à moutons, le matin, which he referred to in a letter as 'mon Clair de Lune avec les moutons' (Fidell-Beaufort and Bailly-Herzberg 1975, p. 265); in 1865, Effet de lune; and in 1868, Lever de lune. For the 1870s, see Hellebranth 1976, nos 349, 377, 408, 411, 414–15, 476, 694, 717, 719, 828, 835, 840, 842, 872, 878, 910–11, 932, 940 and 944–51.

147 He had lunch with Whistler in July 1865 and dinner with him in 1866. Lochnan 2008, p. 49. They probably met also in Trouville; Fidell-Beaufort and Bailly-Herzberg 1975, p. 57.
148 Conservator James Horns believes that it was painted all at one time; Minneapolis, 20 March 1996.
149 Henriet, cited in Laran and Crémieux 1912, p. 112.
150 He was writing about Daubigny's Effet de lune, Salon of 1865; Paul Mantz, cited in Laran and Crémieux 1912, p. 85. See also Mantz 1878, p. 422, on 'l'élimination volontaire du détail … qui implique une sorte de vue synthétique … l'essence même des choses'.
151 Henriet 1874, p. 266. He was alluding to Daubigny's plein-air practice of applying brushstrokes that synthesised light, colour and atmosphere.
152 Brooke 1989, pp. 80–2.
153 Redon, cited in Lemaire 1986, p. 229.
154 Enault 1878, p. 53.
155 Fernandez (1878) 1997, p. 171.
156 See above, n. 78, and Daubigny's letter of 15 October 1854, in Fidell-Beaufort and Bailly-Herzberg 1975, p. 259 n. 1.
157 Letter, 1881, Musée d'Orsay, Aut.351, AR13, p. 88.
158 'La Chanson des foins', in Dupont 1855–9, vol. 3, pp. 169–72.
159 Fidell-Beaufort and Bailly-Herzberg 1975, p. 48.
160 Wickenden 1892, p. 335.
161 'Grimm's Ecstasy' (1991), Stella 2001, pp. 147–51. I thank Robert T. Wallace for calling this text to my attention.
162 Herbert 1981, about Monet and Van Gogh, reprinted 2002, p. 20.
163 Wolff 1886, p. 147.
164 Letter, 27 July 1874; Michel 1904, p. 563.
165 Shiff 2003, pp. 168–9.

DAUBIGNY AND THE IMPRESSIONISTS IN THE 1860S
Maite van Dijk
pp. 45–63

1 Rewald 1946. See also these important publications: Clarke 1986, and Tinterow and Loyrette 1994.
2 Du Camp 1859, p. 161.
3 Castagnary 1892, vol. 1, p. 71.
4 Tinterow and Loyrette 1994, p. 59.
5 Gautier 1859.
6 Duffy 2010, p. 13.
7 Clarke 1986, p. 17.
8 Tinterow and Loyrette 1994, pp. 24–5.
9 The term Impressionism would be used for the first time in 1874 by a critic reviewing the first exhibition these young artists staged together. In this essay the young generation of artists will be referred to as Impressionists even when discussing the period prior to 1874, because they are currently known as such. The term impression was used earlier to indicate a direct and personal reflection of nature, as is clear from the art reviews.
10 Pelloquet 1858, pp. 69–70.
11 See for a discussion of this term the first essay by Lynne Ambrosini in this volume.
12 Moreau-Nélaton 1925, p. 81.
13 Henriet 1875, p. 267.
14 Castagnary 1861, p. 11.

15 Zacharie 1859, pp. 286–7. Pissarro's name appears in the index, which is how we know that this description relates to his entry.

16 Zola 1866, p. 67.

17 See the essay by René Boitelle in this volume for an extensive description of the materials and techniques used in Daubigny's painting.

18 Rewald 1946, p. 312.

19 Privat 1865, p. 190.

20 Gallet 1865, p. 23.

21 Tinterow and Loyrette 1994, p. 86.

22 See also Rothkopf and Lloyd 2007, p. 48.

23 Marlais et al. 2004, p. 45.

24 For more information about Daubigny's boat see the essay by Michael Clarke in this volume.

25 For more information about these contacts see Mitchell 1981, pp. 44–9.

26 This quote is taken from Moffett 1986, p. 93. Moffett dated this letter to 1869, but Dianne Pitman has shown that the letter (no. 83) was written in 1867. Bazille 1992, p. 137.

27 Castagnary 1892, vol. 1, p. 248.

28 Ibid., p. 255.

29 According to a letter from Valabrègue, whose portrait, painted by Cézanne, was one of the submissions. Quoted in Rewald 1946, p. 139.

30 Castagnary 1892, vol. 1, p. 255.

31 Ibid., p. 254. The 'Sainte-Beuve dinner' is a reference to the dinners that had been held every two months at Restaurant Magny since 1862, at which Sainte-Beuve was one of the regular guests. These dinners – which were also attended by Georges Sand, the De Goncourt brothers and Flaubert, among others – were known as a haven of free thinking.

32 Laran and Crémieux 1912, pp. 11–12.

33 Redon [1868] 1986. My thanks to Lynne Ambrosini for drawing this quotation to my attention.

34 See for example Grangedor 1868, p. 27.

35 Auvray 1868, p. 83.

36 Zola 1868.

37 Alexandre 1921, p. 61

38 House 1978, p. 636.

39 Assouline 2004, p. 99.

40 Patry et al. 2014, p. 199.

41 Monet in a letter to Moreau-Nélaton, 14 January 1925. Quoted in House 1978, p. 636.

42 Bonafoux 2008, vol. 2, p. 33.

43 Patry et al. 2014, p. 136.

44 Bakker 1986, p. 102.

45 Letter dated 19 September 1871, quoted in Miquel 1975, p. 698. The painting of the Thames (fig. 45) was likewise not made on the spot. The art dealer Brame commissioned Daubigny to make this work when he was already back in Paris (Amic 2013, p. 296). For more information on the practice of painting outdoors see the essay by René Boitelle in this volume.

46 This is discussed at length in the essays by Michael Clarke and René Boitelle in this volume.

47 Fournel 1884, p. 344.

TALES OF THE RIVERBANK: DAUBIGNY'S RIVER SCENES
Michael Clarke
pp. 65–79

1 Moreau-Nélaton 1925, p. 97.

2 This and the following observations are very much indebted to Robb 2007.

3 Gustave Flaubert, *Sentimental Education* (originally published Paris, 1869), trans. Robert Baldick, London, 1969, pp. 15–16.

4 For a selection of critical reviews see Miquel 1975, pp. 682–4.

5 Delteil 1921, no. 79.

6 See Herbert 1981.

7 Merson 1861, pp. 322–3.

8 Gautier 1861, p. 21.

9 W. Bürger [Théophile Thoré], 'Salon de 1861', reprinted in Thoré-Bürger 1870, vol. 1, p. 53.

10 *Le Tour de Marne, décrit et photographié par Emile de La Bedolière et Ildefonse Rousset*, Paris, 1865, quoted in Kelly 2013, p. 37. As Richard Brettell has observed: 'On occasion the coincidence between a descriptive text in a guidebook and an Impressionist painting is so close that one can scarcely believe that the painter had not read the guide.' Brettell and Schafer 1984, p. 42.

11 This was first pointed out in Clarke 1986, p. 9.

12 Miquel 1975, p. 679 dates the construction of the studio boat to 1856, but offers no evidence for this. However, all other commentators assume this took place in 1857, the year it was launched.

13 See Nonne 2013.

14 Jan van Goyen (1596–1656) was reputed to have had a boat from which he painted. In the early nineteenth century the great English landscape painter J.M.W. Turner (1775–1851) sketched frequently on rivers: for example his principal outdoor sketching campaign in 1805 involved a lengthy boat trip on the Thames from Isleworth to Windsor, along its tributary to Guildford, and back on the Thames as far as Oxford, before continuing downstream; see Brown 1991.

15 Moreau-Nélaton 1925, p. 77.

16 Ibid., p. 74.

17 Quoted in Bomford et al. 1990, p. 26.

18 Originally in a small sketchbook which may have been dismembered by Daubigny himself, their top edges have an uneven dark orange stain, suggesting the binding of the sketchbook may have bled as a result of getting wet on board the *Botin*. They were donated by Moreau-Nélaton to the Louvre in 1927.

19 Fidell 1974.

20 Fidell-Beaufort 2015.

21 Delteil 1921, no. 100.

22 Ibid., no. 101.

23 Ibid., no. 103.

24 Ibid., no. 104.

25 Ibid., no. 106.

26 Ibid., no. 111.

27 On the symbolism of the open window as a motif for artists longing to work out of doors see Eitner 1955.

28 Moreau-Nélaton 1925, p. 77.

29 Tryon 1896, p. 161.

30 Delteil 1921, no. 112.

31 Ibid., no. 114.

32 Ibid., no. 115.

33 Proust 1913, p. 84. Writing in 1904, Emile Michel laid great emphasis on Daubigny's own fondness for water and his desire to study it day and night (Michel 1904, p. 566).

34 Tucker 1984.

35 House 1986, p. 140 n. 27.

36 Kelly 2013.

37 See the second essay by Lynne Ambrosini in this volume.

38 Clarke and Thomson 2003.

39 Galerie Durand-Ruel, Paris, 1878.

40 House 1986, p. 140 n. 27.

41 Ibid.

THE MARKET FOR DAUBIGNY'S LANDSCAPES, OR 'THE BEST PICTURES DO NOT SELL'
Lynne Ambrosini
pp. 81–91

1 *Galerie Durand Ruel: Spécimens les plus brillants de l'école moderne,* 2 vols, Paris, 1845. Daubigny engraved the frontispiece, a view of the gallery interior.

2 This study depends on Daubigny's unpublished correspondence, account books from the Raskin-Daubigny family and the Musée d'Orsay, stock books in the Durand-Ruel Archives and the Goupil Gallery's stock books at the Getty Research Institute. I am very grateful to Anne and the late Daniel Raskin-Daubigny for entrusting me with copies of Daubigny's early account books. I also thank very warmly Paul-Louis Durand-Ruel and Flavie Durand-Ruel for assisting me with research in the Archives Durand-Ruel. Finally, I thank the staffs of the Fondation Custodia, Paris; the Département des Arts Graphiques, Musées d'Orsay et du Louvre, Paris; the Institut National d'Histoire de l'Art, Paris; and the Frick Art Reference Library, New York. On the special status of landscape as 'the prime object of focus for speculation', see Green 1987, p. 67, and Green 1990, pp. 95–110.

3 He moved out of the family home after his mother's death (1834) and father's remarriage (1835). Fidell-Beaufort and Bailly-Herzberg 1975, pp. 32–4.

4 He sent small sums to his wife and children while on painting trips. Ibid., pp. 236–55. Married to Sophie Garnier in 1842, he had three children born in 1843, 1846 and 1853.

5 Letter, 5 October 1843, in Fidell-Beaufort and Bailly-Herzberg 1975, p. 249. The letters also reveal a humorous, enthusiastic and buoyant personality.

6 Melot 1980, p. 281, D.111, from the series *Le Voyage en bateau*.

7 See the letter from Daubigny about an illustration commission, Fondation Custodia, 1977-A.198.

8 Zola (June 1876); Fernandez 1997, p. 170. The prices recorded in the earliest known account book (beginning in 1856) validate Zola's claim. Account Books (Raskin-Daubigny), pp. 2, 8, 9.

9 See Théodore Duret's 1874 counsel to Pissarro that to become well known he had only two main avenues, 'the auctions at the Hôtel Drouot and the big exhibition at the Palais d'Industrie [the Salon]'. House 1995, p. 26.

10 Société des Artistes Français, *Explication des ouvrages de peintures …* , Paris, 1857, p. 81, nos 688–90.

11 Jules Claretie found 'huge defects' in the *Barrelmaker*: the paint was piled on so thickly and stuck out so far that one could easily hang something from it. 'How much,' he went on, 'I prefer to this *Barrelmaker* the painting that Mr Daubigny names "Mills at Dordrecht" … it is a masterpiece of colour and charm.' Claretie 1874, pp. 231–2. The painting surfaced on the New York art market in 2013–14 and sold to private collectors; it is illustrated at www.schillerandbodo.com/artists/Daubigny. For a sketch by Daubigny after the Salon of 1872 painting, see Moreau-Nélaton 1925, fig. 91, opposite p. 103.

12 Daguet 1971, p. 33.

13 Fidell-Beaufort and Bailly-Herzberg 1975, p. 50. Daubigny advised Corot on marketing, Pantazzi 1996, p. 397–8.

14 Anon. 1868. At an exhibition in Marseille in 1869, he exhibited a *Vue d'automne à Anvers* [sic], probably 'Auvers'; see Ravenel 1869a, pp. 126–7. Daubigny exhibited in Bordeaux the same year; Ravenel 1869b, p. 256.

15 Led by the painter and dealer Louis Martinet; see Huston 1990, pp. 45–50.

16 Account Books (Raskin-Daubigny), p. 16, called 'Les Varech' (kelp or seaweed). Daubigny illustrated it in ink and wrote

'les vareck [sic], Exposé au boulevard des Italiens en Janvier 1862, refusé à l'Exposition en 1855'.

17 Thoré 1870, vol. 1, pp. 289–90. The painting is not yet identified, as is the case for many pictures mentioned here.

18 Thomson 1890, p. 278. Thomson added that as early as 1854 an English painter, G.P. Boyce, had purchased a Daubigny landscape of Villerville. In 1866, *Moonlight* (also shown at the Salon of 1865, current location unknown), was hung very high; Thompson reported that a British painter named H.T. Well purchased it from the exhibition.

19 Account Book (Musée d'Orsay), Aut.367b, AR16, p. 4 verso.

20 Letter, 3 August 1852, in Fidell-Beaufort and Bailly-Herzberg 1975, p. 257.

21 Letter, 9 September 1876, Musée d'Orsay, Aut.363, AR14, p. 29.

22 Haskell 1982, pp. 40–7.

23 Museum der bildenden Künste 2003, pp. 73–5. The exhibition was arranged by the dealer Paul Détrimont. See Bouillon 1986, p. 93.

24 *Explication des ouvrages de peinture … Salon de 1863*, Paris, 1863, no. 513. Account Books (Raskin-Daubigny), p. 26. Daubigny, having set the price at 5,000 francs, must have accepted a lower price; Moreau-Nélaton 1925, pp. 83–4; also Kelly 2013, p. 166.

25 Account Books (Raskin-Daubigny), 1868, p. 49. He sold the painting for 2,000 francs. Larrieu, who was the owner of a leading vineyard, Château Haut-Brion, in Bordeaux, later became Prefect of the Gironde. By the 1870s, collectors came to Daubigny's studio from far and wide; witness commissions from 'M. Bogaluboff de St. Petersbourg' and 'M. Dudley Williams, Boston'. Account Book (Musée d'Orsay), Aut.367b, AR16, p. 65 recto and verso.

26 Account Books (Raskin-Daubigny), the painting sold for 2,500 francs in 1858, p. 16. The Doria sale catalogue included three other Daubignys: *Une vallée*, *Vue prise près de Château-Chinon*, and *Un coin de bois*; *Collection de M. le Comte Armand Doria, Tableaux Modernes*, Paris, Petit et al., 1899, vol. 2, p. 82, nos 124–6.

27 Nadar bought Daubigny's *Banks of the Oise* (fig. 050) for 5,000 francs and commissioned a second painting, *La Frette*, a site on the Seine, also in 1859. Account Books (Raskin-Daubigny), 1859, p. 21. In London in 1865, Daubigny sold a small *Lever de lune à Optevoz* to Leighton ('M. Leiton') for 600 francs and *Thames* to Seymour Haden (written 'Eyden') for 1,200 francs. Account Books (Raskin-Daubigny), 1865, pp. 29, 34. He sold two works to the British painter Barbara Bodichon, *Conflans* and *Villerville*, for 800 and 600 francs respectively on 22 December 1865; Account Books (Raskin-Daubigny), 1865, p. 28. Alexandre Dumas owned Daubigny's *Les Ruines de Château-Gaillard*, 1873; Hellebranth 1976, no. 89. On 9 June 1877, Daubigny mentioned having sold another painting, 'le Clair de lune', to Dumas fils. Letter, Musée d'Orsay, Aut.364, AR14, p. 31. Daubigny's friend and employer, the publisher and draughtsman Giacomelli, served as intermediary in 1870 for a commission from Jules Janin for a *Bords de l'Oise*. Letter, Fondation Custodia, 1977-A.199 and 1977-A.200.

28 After Mesdag inherited his father's fortune in 1881, he set about avidly collecting progressive French art. Opening his museum in 1887, he announced, 'I have 25 Daubignys… .'. His taste for Daubigny's most adventurous works – broadly painted and large – was unusual for its time. See Van Dijk et al. 2015, pp. 77–8, 83, 95, 97.

29 The undated letter probably dates from about 1866, based on the prices. Institut National d'Histoire de l'Art, carton 10, nos 443–4. In another undated letter to an unknown dealer, Daubigny wrote, 'Dear Sir, in case of sales, here are the most recent prices of my paintings. The apple

tree, 2,000 [francs], the marine painting, 1,200 [francs], the little river 1,500 [francs] …' Getty Research Institute (870475).

30 Account Books (Raskin-Daubigny), 1868, p. 36; sales to the Hungarian Count János Pálffy.

31 Durand-Ruel 1939, pp. 165–6.

32 Account Book (Musée d'Orsay), AR367b, AR16, p. 4 verso; this sold to Goupil. In his last years, pressed by his dealers, Daubigny opened his Paris studio to visitors one day a week; he found talking to them wearying; Wolff 1883, p. 70.

33 This holds true for Millet's mature years. I thank Alexandra Murphy for this information.

34 Compiling their names from the surviving account books only, which may under-represent their numbers, yields: Adolphe Beugniet, A. Binant, A. Bourges, Léon Boussod, Hector Brame, Breysse, Alfred Cadart, Claudon, Cléophas, Colcombe, Paul Détrimont, Paul Durand-Ruel, Duval, Estienne, Fréret, Ernest Gambart, Alphonse Giroux, Adolphe Goupil, Grédeluc, Klein, Louis Latouche, George A. Lucas, Pierre-Ferdinand ('Père') Martin, Louis Martinet, Louis Mayer, Ottoz, Painel, Poignant, Poirat, Schenk, Charles Sedelmeyer, Surville, Tedesco, Tempelaere, Thérault, Georges Thomas, Seth Vose and Emmanuel Weyl. Account Books (Raskin-Daubigny and Musée d'Orsay).

35 For example, the paint merchant Colcombe bought six paintings from Daubigny between 1858 and 1864; Account Books (Raskin-Daubigny), p. 20. The gilder Grédelue ordered five paintings in 1868; ibid., p. 52. Louis Latouche, an artist, paint-supplier and dealer, purchased four paintings from Daubigny in 1868 and another six in 1869; ibid., p. 43bis. Finally, Daubigny's print editor, Alfred Cadart, commissioned eight small paintings from him when they travelled to London together in 1865; ibid., p. 29. See also Nonne 2010, pp. 363–73.

36 Duplessis 1856, p. 290. Beugniet first listed his frame-making business in 1847 in the Paris directory. *Annuaire-Almanach du Commerce* (Bottin 1840–78) as 'encadreur d'estampes et tableaux, rue Laffitte, 18'. In the 1867 directory Beugniet gave a more complete listing: 'Vente et location de tableaux modernes, spécialité d'encadrements artistiques, dépôt d'eaux-fortes et seul dépôt de bronzes de Barye'. See Henriet 1854, pp. 113–15; and Constantin 2001, pp. 51, 62.

37 This is true for each of the years for which we have account books. Account Books (Raskin-Daubigny), pp. 12, 13, 26, 33, 44. Account Books (Musée d'Orsay), Aut.367b, AR16, pp. 52–4.

38 Letter, dated Monday, 19 May 1863, Institut National d'Histoire de l'Art, carton 10, no. 428.

39 This was the expensive end of Beugniet's range for the late 1860s. The low end was 800 francs. Account Books (Raskin-Daubigny), p. 44. Other dealers who worked in the middle to lower range of Daubigny's market included Bourges, Latouche, Surville, Tedesco, Tempelaere and Weyl.

40 Lucas 1979, vol. 2, p. 146. Soon after we read of his first Daubigny purchases: 'Tuesday 10 Feb. 1863, at Hotel D[rouot] & brought drawing of Daubigny'; 'Fri. 27 Nov. 1863, At Daubigny's where met Bonvin; at Petits & bought small Daubigny for W[alter]'s for 600 francs.' Ibid., vol. 2, pp. 150, 166.

41 Account Books (Raskin-Daubigny), 1863, p. 26. Lucas recorded: 'Thursday 4 Feb. 1864. Gave Daubigny an order for 2 small landscapes the [two] 2,900 francs'; Lucas 1979, vol. 2, p. 171.

42 Lucas 1979, vol. 2, pp. 171–90. After Walters's return to the United States in 1865, Lucas's visits to Daubigny slowed to once or twice a year; ibid., vol. 2, pp. 243, 264 and 383.

43 Also Cyrus J. Lawrence, Frank Frick and Henry Field; Frick Archives http://research.frick.org/directoryweb/browserecord.php?-action=browse&-recid=6947.

44 Vose 1993, pp. 3–4. Later the gallery moved to Boston.

45 Tryon 1896, p. 156.

46 Sedelmeyer had a gallery at 54 Faubourg Montmartre from 1866 and a gallery in Vienna; Wild 1994, pp. 76–80.

47 Account Book (Musée d'Orsay), called there 'Le clair de lune et le joueur de flute', Aut.367b, AR16, pp. 22–3. The third painting commissioned in November 1872 was a *Bords de l'Oise*, for 3,000 francs. In December 1873, Sedelmeyer ordered another three paintings for 3,000 to 3,500 francs apiece. On the history of the *Lever de lune* in the Budapest Museum, see Rózsa-Kaposy 1979, pp. 170–1, and Illyés 2001, pp. 62–3.

48 Account Book (Musée d'Orsay), Aut.367b, AR16, p. 1. Little is known about Breysse, including his first name.

49 Ibid., p. 1 verso. *La Neige* measures about 3 feet high by 6 feet wide. Daubigny recorded the order for *Moonlight* as 'Clair de lune, tableau de la grandeur Dordrecht'. Breysse also ordered smaller paintings, adding up to a total of twenty-four pictures over a three-year period. Ibid., p. 1 verso.

50 A good succinct history of the international firm is found in the British Museum's Biography index. http://www.britishmuseum.org/research/search_the_collection_database/term_details.aspx?bioId=123112. On the firm's early years, see Burty 1867, p. 96. See also Fletcher and Helmreich 2011, pp. 65–84.

51 Whitely 2002, p. 102.

52 Saglio 1860, pp. 46, 52.

53 Account Book (Musée d'Orsay), Aut.367b, AR16, p. 4 verso.

54 Goupil Archives (2823-978). The average price of the Daubigny paintings Goupil's sold in the 1870s was 3,273 francs. By contrast, the firm had sold five paintings by Daubigny in the 1860s, at an average price of 782 francs. I thank Taft curatorial assistant Katie G. Benedict for her assistance with research and Finance director Beth K. Siler for help with financial analysis of the dealers' transactions.

55 Daubigny's annual *direct* sales to Goupil included thirty paintings between 1871 and 1874, as follows: in 1871, ten paintings for a total of 32,500 francs; in 1872, seven paintings (some larger) totalling 44,000 francs; in 1873 seven paintings for 37,000 francs; in 1874, six, for 16,000 francs. Account Book (Musée d'Orsay), p. 4 recto and verso.

56 Goupil's sold his works to buyers named Tuckermann, Stewart, Morton, Ledge, Brandeis, Greene Hubbard Gardiner (Boston), Adolph Kohn (New York), Chapman, Lepke (Berlin), Sergei Mikhailovich Tretyakov, Polovtstoff, Mesdag (The Hague) and Mietke (Vienna). As for sales to dealers, in the 1870s Goupil's sold ten paintings to Knoedler's and one to Samuel P. Avery in New York. In London, they sold three to Wallis & Sons, four to Everard & Co., three to MacLean's and three to Cottier. Goupil Archives (2823-978).

57 Purchase date 13 January 1873, sale date 21 January 1873, to a Mr Goldschmidt. Goupil Stock Book 6, no. 7534, Goupil Archives (2823-978). A more typical margin was achieved on a work they purchased from Daubigny's 1878 estate sale for 840 francs and sold to H.M. Mesdag thirteen months later for 1,600 francs. Goupil Stock Book 9, no. 12670, purchase date 6 April 1878; sale date 15 May 1879. Goupil Archives (2823-978).

58 Goupil's purchased it on 1 December 1877 and sold it to Secrétan on 23 June 1880; Goupil Stock Book 10, no. 12385, Goupil Archives (2823-978).

59 Champier 1878, p. 172.

60 Goupil's sold 215 works from 1879 to 1889 at an average price of 8,019 francs. Goupil Archives (2823-978).

61 In his lifetime, dealers bought a wide range of his subjects; Account Books (Raskin-Daubigny). Those who dealt with lower price points did, however, show some preference for river pictures with their certain turnaround.

62 In the first decade of the twentieth century, the percentage of the river views in his sales stayed high at 59 per cent. Goupil Archives, records of sales of Daubigny analysed by decade; Getty Research Institute (2823-978).

63 The earliest currently known account book begins in 1856; Account Books (Raskin-Daubigny). One example of Durand-Ruel's support of Daubigny's work at auctions was a small *Seine à Herblay* that he purchased at a public sale on 23 March 1868, for 685 francs, and sold for a loss at 650 francs on 16 December 1868. Archives Durand-Ruel, Paris, stock book, 'Tableaux (et dessins) achetés de moitié avec M. Brame, 1866–1872'.

64 On the dealer's early career, see Patry *et al.* 2014, notably the essays by Paul-Louis and Flavie Durand-Ruel and by Simon Kelly.

65 Durand-Ruel 1939a, pp. 163–4. Hector Brame began his career as an actor with a penchant for art, but left the theatre to open his own gallery in the rue Taitbout in 1864. See Distel 1990, p. 36, and Whitely 2014.

66 In that decade, Daubigny's sales to the two dealers amounted to 34,200 francs. Account Books (Raskin-Daubigny), pp. 26, 30, 39, 40.

67 Henriet 1891, pp. 72–3. After Daubigny's death, the furniture and supplies in the studio were valued at 1,440 francs, so these were not terribly costly accoutrements. See 'Inventory of Houses, Studio, and Paris Apartment', in Fidell-Beaufort and Bailly Herzberg 1975, pp. 267–73.

68 In 1868–72, they paid Daubigny 106,900 francs, according to his account books, effectively tripling their purchases of 1857–67. Sometime in 1871 or early 1872 they stopped making joint purchases.

69 After 1872, both Daubigny's account books and the Durand-Ruel stock books are incomplete. Daubigny's records for 1873–8 are missing, though he noted sales to a few dealers in 1873 and 1874 in the Musée d'Orsay account book. There are no Durand-Ruel stock books for the period 1872–5.

70 Account Books (Raskin-Daubigny), 1869, p. 43.

71 Exhibited at the Salon as *Evening at Andrésy (Banks of the Seine)*, s.d., 1866. Brame commissioned it in 1865 for 1,200 francs. Account Books (Raskin-Daubigny), p. 30; Daubigny recorded it as 'Andresy, lever de lune'.

72 Account Book (Musée d'Orsay), Aut.367b, AR16, p. 27. There is no record in Durand-Ruel's stock books of the sale of this painting because it was a solo purchase by Brame. See Moreau-Nélaton 1925, p. 109. It entered the collection of G. Norman, Newport, RI, later; Hellebranth 1976, p. 161, no. 498. See note 11.

73 Daubigny recorded this price in 1869; with the dislocations of the war years, he may not have dated the painting until after the war, in 1871. In some other instances, he appears to have dated pictures at the point of sale, using the current year. Account Books (Raskin-Daubigny), 1869, p. 43.

74 See the essay by Maite van Dijk in this volume.

75 Green 1987, pp. 59–67, 72, 74. Also, Godfroy 2000, pp. 82–90.

76 At least three articles praised his work: Raffey 1869, p. 485; Ravenel 1870, p. 321; Anon. 1870, p. 76, which exhorted Philadelphians to compete with New Yorkers in the realm of art collecting and pointed out the safety of purchasing securely attributed works by Daubigny and other contemporary artists (whom Durand-Ruel handled).

77 The catalogue and etchings were ready in January 1873 but never published. A few proofs exist. Venturi 1939a, vol. 1, pp. 18–19.

78 Daubigny recorded the commission from Breysse for 4,500 francs in 1871. Account Book (Musée d'Orsay), Aut.367b, AR16, p. 1. Durand-Ruel recorded the purchase 13 February 1873 with a different title, 'Bateaux et moulins en Hollande', but the measurements match Breysse's picture. Durand-Ruel Archives, stock book, 'Tableaux 1876'.

79 *Crépuscule*, Durand-Ruel Archives, stock book, 'Stock 1866–70'.

80 Stock books, Durand-Ruel Archives. Like Goupil, Durand-Ruel bought works by Daubigny from many sources – auctions, private sales, and other dealers – not just from the artist.

81 Gambart and a few other dealers offered French art, including Daubigny's work, for sale in London before Durand-Ruel's arrival there in autumn, 1870. Durand-Ruel had earlier sold pictures by Daubigny to the London dealer Thomas MacLean; for example, Daubigny's *Bords de l'Oise*, purchased from Samuel P. Avery, the New York dealer, for 2,000 francs in 1868, and sold to MacLean, March 1869, for 2,250 francs. He sold another Oise subject to MacLean in May 1869, with a similar mark-up. Durand-Ruel Archives, stock book, 'Stock 1866–70'.

82 Thomson 2000, p. 80.

83 He had shipped all his stock to London; Durand-Ruel 1939, pp. 175–6.

84 For the committee, he named artists he supported, who would not have minded. Anne Robbins cites a letter that Durand-Ruel wrote to Fromentin, explaining the committee as a way to give the exhibition an artistic stamp and to 'faire oublier le côté commercial;' 'A la Conquête de Londres', in Patry *et al.* 2014, p. 138.

85 'The First Annual Exhibition in London of pictures'. 'The contribution of the Society of French Artists ... 168 New Bond Street. Committee: DAUBIGNY ... , 1871.' This information was graciously provided by Flavie Durand-Ruel.

86 Each exhibition included a mix of Daubigny's motifs with no more than one or two river scenes in each. Overall, the thirty or so paintings were comprised of one-third river views (the Seine, the Oise and the Cure), one-third scenes of rural life that would have been attractive to the British (flowering orchards, farm fields, pastures with livestock, marshes and cottages), and one-third views of striking sites in Holland, Normandy and London. The number of thirty is approximate because the 10 December 1870 catalogue, the 'First Annual Exhibition', is so hard to find that it may not actually have been published. It could have been a first version of the identically titled 'First Annual Exhibition' that opened in early 1871; see n. 84, above. If the December 1870 show was different and included one work by Daubigny, then the total number of works by him exhibited in all the shows would be thirty.

87 From the *First Annual Exhibition*, 1871, no. 46, *Evening*. Precise identification of the paintings is hampered by the fact that they are given without dimensions, descriptions, or dates, and the English titles do not match known French titles. Only two paintings can be identified with any certainty: Daubigny's *St Paul's, from the Surrey Side*, in the *Eighth Exhibition*, 1874, no. 41 (National Gallery, London, fig. 021); and also *The Barrelmaker* from the *Ninth Exhibition*, 1874, no. 97, (fig. 123), commissioned by Durand-Ruel and Brame in 1871 for 10,000 francs and shown at the Salon of 1872. As records of sales from the London exhibitions do not survive, we cannot measure their impact.

88 Durand-Ruel 1939, p. 180. *International Exhibition, Official Catalogue. Fine Arts Department*, London, 1871, unpaginated, East Galleries, Rooms XIX and XX, nos 1183–91 and 1344. Five paintings listed as being from the collection of the artist may have come from Durand-Ruel's stock; one of them matches a picture sold to Brame and Durand-Ruel in 1868: *Banks of the Cure, in Morvan*, 1867, Account Books

(Raskin-Daubigny), p. 40. In a display representing France, Durand-Ruel did not include Daubigny's pictures of London. Four of Daubigny's nine pictures already came from British collections, specifically those of James Staats Forbes, the railway entrepreneur, a Mr Wells, and Hugh Grosvenor, the Marquess of Westminster. Forbes owned *Shades of Evening*, 1861, and *Sunset*, 1861, nos 1186–7. *Moonlight – Picardy* belonged to Mr Wells and *Sunset – near Pontoise* to the 'Marquis of Westminster', nos 1188 and 1191. It was about this time that Durand-Ruel sold another Daubigny, a Villerville coastal view, to Forbes, and one to a Mr Musard in London. *Soleil couchant à Villerville* was purchased from Daubigny for 2,500 francs and sold to Forbes for 3,125 francs, while *L'étang*, purchased from Daubigny in London for 1,600 francs, sold for 2,500 francs, probably to Alfred Musard (1828–1881), a popular conductor. Durand-Ruel Archives, stock books, 'Stock 1866–70' and 'Tableaux 1876'.

89 It was from the period of Durand-Ruel's stay in London that many of the leading British collections of 'Barbizon' art were formed. Whitely 2002, p. 101. Durand-Ruel's parting salute to Daubigny and all the recently deceased landscapists came in the form of a retrospective exhibition held at his Paris gallery a few months after Daubigny's death in February 1878. This was to redress what he perceived as the shortcomings of the Exposition Universelle of 1878 that summer. The gallery show included eighteen paintings by Daubigny; Galerie Durand-Ruel 1878, p. 30.

90 Dated 1863. Fowle 2006, p. 144. See also Watson 2008, p. 195.

91 Goupil's sold thirty-five Daubigny paintings to British buyers then; Goupil Archives (2823-978).

92 Green 1990, pp. 198–6. See also House 1995, p. 27.

93 Henriet 1881, vol. 25, p. 82.

94 Castagnary 1892, vol. 1, p. 145.

95 *La pêche aux écrevisses*, Account Books (Raskin-Daubigny), 1867, p. 50. No price is given. This is probably the title that Daubigny would have given to the National Gallery's *Willows*, too.

96 *La pêche aux écrevisses, soleil levant*, Account Book (Musée d'Orsay), Aut.367b, AR16, pp. 24–5.

97 *La pêche aux écrevisses*, Account Book (Musée d'Orsay), Aut.367b, AR16, pp. 17–18. Cléophas paid for it on 9 April 1872. This is probably Hellebranth 1996, no. 161. It is more precise in its handling than the National Gallery work.

98 Comparing the last digit to Daubigny's habitually rounded '2's, I read the last digit as a '4'. Davies 1970, pp. 42–3.

99 In 1867/8, Daubigny recorded an order for the dealer Surville as 'répétition de matin Palffy', naming a collector.

100 'Sujet de M. Bogaluboff, sujet Oudinot, sujet Brame.' Account Book (Musée d'Orsay), Aut. 367b, AR16, pp. 59–60.

101 Zola (1866) 1991, p. 132.

102 Wolff 1883, p. 70.

103 Tryon 1896, p. 165.

104 His will left explicit instructions that upon his death, his wife was to sell at public auction all his paintings, studies and drawings, after first making a choice among them for herself. 'Testament de M. Daubigny', in Fidell-Beaufort and Bailly-Herzberg 1975, p. 271. When Daubigny died in February 1878, Brame served as appraiser and auctioneer for the sale of the atelier's contents. Hôtel Drouot 1878. The market for landscape paintings in Paris was depressed at that time because of the recent deaths and sales of Millet, Corot and Diaz, all between 1875 and 1879. Durand-Ruel said that 1878 marked the nadir; Venturi 1939a, vol. 2, p. 204. So Daubigny's estate sale of 671 lots brought his family much less than expected, only 239,000 francs. Ironically, the large canvases 'for his family' sold for low prices or not at all. For example, the *Parc au Moutons (effet de lune)*, 1878, which

measured 170 × 308 cm and was one of the paintings Tryon admired, sold for only 1,800 francs; Hôtel Drouot 1878, p. 63, no. 457.

105 Durand-Ruel reported that collectors wanted his 'Banks of the Oise' above all else and that in his late years Daubigny had begun to paint them too quickly. Venturi 1939a, vol. 2, p. 186.

106 Henriet 1881, p. 82. Both Henriet and Tryon described some shortcuts that Daubigny took in his late years to create minor pictures rapidly for the market. Henriet 1881, p. 82, and Tryon 1896, p. 164. This practice ultimately hurt his reputation, an effect that has lingered as these small pictures continue to circulate in the market today.

107 The third property in Auvers, on which Daubigny had taken out a mortgage in 1875, had a building with seven apartments, three of them rented. He and his wife had recently been making improvements to it. The other two were the studio-plus-five rooms and kitchen that the Daubignys had built in 1860–2, and a contiguous property they had purchased in 1870 with a barn and chicken coop, to which they had added a small two-storey house. See 'Inventory of Houses … '; Fidell-Beaufort and Bailly-Herzberg 1975, pp. 267–73.

108 Between 1856 and 1859, Daubigny earned 44,200 francs from the sale of his paintings; Account Books (Raskin-Daubigny). His expenses included the rental of an apartment and a separate studio, and support for his family. Even the shabbiest working-class housing in Paris was expensive in 1855: a six-room apartment in a run-down building rented for 1,800 francs per month, or 21,600 francs annually. Shapiro 1985, p. 38. Daubigny and his family must have had a hard time making ends meet. Between 1860 and 1866, Daubigny began to earn more, making a total of 80,650 francs. The sharpest increase in his income occurred beginning in 1867: between then and 1869 alone, he earned 215,800 francs. Over the course of 1860s, he earned a total of 296,450 francs, two-thirds of it raised in the preceding three years. Against that, he had assumed the expenses of the property in Auvers, the construction of a house and studio there, and the maintenance of the studio boat and house.

109 To understand Daubigny's prices in terms of salaries of the day, see Reverdy 1973, pp. 41–52 and Appendix 4, 'Daubigny', pp. 147–58. The peak of his market was just before the First World War. I mention 1871 to 1873 because these are the only years in that decade for which we have good records. Account Book (Musée d'Orsay), Aut.367b, AR16. That account book can be deceiving in one respect: Daubigny appears to have begun it after the Franco-Prussian War and Commune, but in it he *re-recorded* many works that had already been commissioned and for which payments had been made in the late 1860s (already recorded in the earlier Raskin-Daubigny account books). Perhaps Daubigny had lost or misplaced the earlier books and was trying to reconstitute them. If these repetitions are not eliminated, the numbers of paintings and relevant earnings in 1871–3 appear inflated. For this reason, a fine recent article contained an inadvertent overstatement of Daubigny's earnings from sales of paintings in 1871 (Kelly 2013, p. 36.) After Daubigny returned to Paris in the summer of 1871, his earnings for *new commissions* during the rest of the year actually totalled only 59,200 francs. (In turn, the figures that I give here will need to be revised in future, when missing account books come to light.) Further, it is difficult to be sure that 'Daubigny continued in that manner [i.e. earning comparable amounts] until his death … in 1878', because few records for 1874–8 are available, and Daubigny was intermittently quite ill during that period. Kelly 2013, pp. 36–7.

110 See the summary of Monet's finances in House 1986, p. 11, which is based on the artist's account books preserved in the Museé Marmottan, Paris.

AUVERS-SUR-OISE AS AN ARTISTS' COLONY: FROM DAUBIGNY TO VAN GOGH
Frances Fowle
pp. 93–103

1 On this see, for example, Thoré 1847; Thoré 1845; and Simon 1890, discussed in Green 1990, pp. 67–71, 74–5, 80, 93.

2 On European artists' colonies see Jacobs 1985, Lübbren 2001 and Barrett 2010. None of these authors discusses Auvers.

3 On Pont-Aven, Crozant and Giverny see Pickvance 1994; Fowle 2013; Bourguignon 2007.

4 Joanne 1856, p. 470.

5 It was sold in 1667 to Jean de Lérit and later transformed into a French-style residence.

6 Mataigne 1985, p. 19.

7 Joanne 1856, p. 470.

8 Défossez 1986, p. 2.

9 Fidell-Beaufort and Bailly-Herzberg 1975, p. 31. The cottage features in several of Daubigny's paintings of the early 1870s, for example, *My Nurse's Cottage*, c. 1871, The Mesdag Collection, The Hague; the *House of Mère Bazot, Valmondois*, 1872, Museum of Fine Arts, Boston, and the *House of Mère Bazot*, 1874, Art Institute of Chicago.

10 Miquel 1975, pp. 667, 672–3.

11 Moreau-Nélaton 1905, p. 159.

12 Zola 1876.

13 Auvray, cited in Miquel 1975, p. 682.

14 Anon. 1990.

15 Much of the information in this section is based on Gachet 1990, p. 184.

16 Gachet 1990, p. 184. See also Daubigny's letter to Geoffroy-Dechaume in Miquel 1975, p. 684.

17 An illustrated account of the decoration at the Villa des Vallées is given in Léonide Bourges *Daubigny: Souvenirs et Croquis* with a preface by Roger Milès, Paris 1894 (Cabinet des Estampes, Bibliothèque Nationale de France, Paris); see also Anon. 1990.

18 Gachet lists the following as the main visitors to the Villa des Vallées: Français, Henri-Joseph Harpignies, Hector Hanoteau, Henriet, Auguste Allongé, Jules Dupré (known as 'le solitaire de l'Isle d'Adam'), Pierre-Emmanuel Damoye, Antoine Guillemet, Pierret (father and son), Lucien-Victor Delpy, Marcellin de Groisseilliez, Léon Germain Pelouse and Berthe Morisot. Gachet 1990, p. 185.

19 Fourreau 1925, p. 21. Edma also submitted a river scene in the manner of Corot.

20 Oil on canvas, 33 × 46 cm, with Galerie Bale, Marion, MA, in 2012.

21 Hellebranth 1976 lists *Le retour des vignerons, Valmondois*, n.d. (no. 202); *Chargement du raisin, Auvers*, c. 1860, atelier sale, 1878 (no. 106); and *Auvers, la vendange*, 1866, atelier sale, 1878 (no. 195). I am grateful to Lynne Ambrosini for pointing out that the Dijon painting, identified by Hellebranth as of Auvers, is almost certainly a study for *The Grape Harvest in the Bourgogne* of 1863 (fig. 102).

22 The latter possible shows the influence of the Barbizon artist Charles Jacque, who was one of several artists to visit Daubigny at Auvers.

23 Hellebranth 1976, no. 145. This was close to where a new railway station would be constructed in 1886. See also Hellebranth 1976, nos 146–7.

24 On Oller see Distel and Stein 1999, p. 128.

25 Domergue 1954. The second house and studio were converted from a grange used for pigs and chickens. See 'Inventaire après décès de Charles F. Daubigny', in Fidell-Beaufort and Bailly-Herzberg 1975, p. 272. Daubigny

spent some time renovating and extending the third house, but died before he was able to move in. See ibid. I am grateful to Lynne Ambrosini for clarifying this for me.

26 On Beauverie see Duvivier 2007, pp. 14–15.

27 Léonide Bourges moved to Auvers in 1874. The daughter of an art dealer, she not only collected Daubigny's works, but compiled a souvenir album, with a detailed account of the building of the Villa des Vallées. See n. 17 above, and Duvivier 2007, pp. 30–1.

28 In 1866, for example, when Cézanne's *Portrait of Antony Valabrègue* (National Gallery of Art, Washington DC) was rejected at the Salon of 1866 Daubigny had tried to intervene on the younger artist's behalf. Danchev 2012, p. 110.

29 The visit is commemorated by a dated still life (Musée d'Orsay), painted at Gachet's house. Cézanne produced a still life with same cloth in background the following year. On Murer see Distel 1989, pp. 207–15.

30 Distel and Stein 1999, p. 6.

31 Distel 1989, p. 212. See also Colin B. Bailey in Stein and Miller 2009, p. 111. Distel 1989, p. 212.

32 Colin B. Bailey in Stein and Miller 2009, pp. 112–13.

33 Ibid.

34 See Rewald *et al*. 1996, p. 66, no. 195. See also Distel and Stein 1999.

35 Ibid., nos 190–4, 202.

36 On Cadart see Jensen 1994, p. 86.

37 According to Venturi, the subject was suggested by Dr Gachet. See Venturi 1936, p. 288, no. 1159.

38 Distel and Stein 1999, p. 124. Gachet had had some of his prints published in the same magazine.

39 Rewald *et al*. 1996, no. 196. There are examples of this print in the Musée Pissarro, Pontoise and the National Museum, Stockholm.

40 Denis Coutagne, 'Le paysage entre Ile-de-France et Provence', in Coutagne *et al*. 2012, p. 210.

41 On this see Fowle 2003.

42 Gachet 1956, p. 56.

43 Venturi 1939b, vol. 1, p. 445.

44 Brettell and Fonsmark 2005, pp. 175–7.

45 On Pearce see Thompson 1993 and Lublin 1993.

46 Alexis 1971. I am grateful to Richard Thomson for pointing out this reference.

47 Letter 172 from Paul Alexis to Emile Zola, 23 August 1887, in Bakker 1971, p. 340. He was staying 'chez M. Sanders' in the rue Rémy.

48 Letter 875, to Theo and Jo van Gogh-Bonger, Auvers, 25 May 1890.

49 Letter 873, to Theo and Jo van Gogh-Bonger, Auvers, 20 May 1890.

IN DAUBIGNY'S FOOTSTEPS: VINCENT VAN GOGH
Nienke Bakker
pp. 105–29

1 Letter 142, to Theo van Gogh, Amsterdam, 3 March 1878. All quotations from Van Gogh's correspondence are from Jansen, Luijten and Bakker 2009, also available online at www.vangoghletters.org.

2 For an extensive chronology of Van Gogh's life, see http://vangoghletters.org/vg/chronology.html.

3 Letter 17, to Theo van Gogh, London, early January 1874.

4 See the second essay by Lynne Ambrosini in this volume.

5 Letter 55, to Theo van Gogh, Paris, 11 October 1875.

6 The scrapbook, now in the Van Gogh Museum, contains forty-two cut-out prints, including lithographs of Daubigny's

La grande vallée d'Optevoz (Salon 1857, Hellebranth 1976, no. 523) and *La rentrée du berger, effet de clair de lune* (Hellebranth 1997, no. 177).

7   Letter 37, to Theo van Gogh, Paris, 6 July 1875, and letter 158, to Theo van Gogh, Cuesmes, 24 September 1880. Van Gogh knew Henriet's book, *Charles Daubigny et son oeuvre gravé* (Henriet 1875), as we learn from letter 133, so he had a good idea of Daubigny's prints. There is no known drawing of *The Bush* by Van Gogh; almost all the drawings of the early years have been lost.

8   For an overview of Van Gogh's preferences, see Stolwijk 2003, and Bakker and Van Dijk 2013. The terms used by Van Gogh were part of the standard vocabulary of nineteenth-century art and literature criticism.

9   Letter 841, to Willemien van Gogh, Saint-Rémy, 20 January 1890. On Van Gogh's perception of nature see Stolwijk 2003.

10 Letter 256, to Anthon van Rappard, The Hague, 13 August 1882. The exhibition was staged in the Academy of Fine Arts in The Hague in July 1882 and contained French art in private collections, including that of the painter Hendrik Willem Mesdag.

11 Letter 246, to Theo van Gogh, The Hague, 15 and 16 July 1882.

12 During his stay in the asylum in Saint-Rémy he made several paintings of thatched cottages from memory, which he called 'reminiscences of Brabant' (see letter 864).

13 Letter 361, to Theo van Gogh, on or about 11 July 1883.

14 Letter 369, to Theo van Gogh, 29 and 30 July 1883.

15 Letter 381, to Theo van Gogh, on or about 5 September 1883.

16 Letter 392, to Theo van Gogh, Nieuw-Amsterdam, on or about 3 October 1883; letter 393, to Theo van Gogh, Nuenen, on or about 7 October 1883.

17 Letter 439, to Anthon van Rappard, Nuenen, on or about 18 March 1884.

18 Letter 537, to Theo van Gogh, Nuenen, on or about 28 October 1885. This 'romantic' view of art was later to put Van Gogh on a collision course with Gauguin, who stayed with him in Arles in the autumn of 1888. Gauguin wrote to Emile Bernard about it: 'In general, Vincent and I see eye to eye on very little, especially on painting. He admires Daudet, Daubigny, Ziem and the great Rousseau, all of them people I can't stand. And on the other hand, he detests Ingres, Raphael, Degas, all of them people whom I admire; I reply, you're right, soldier, for the sake of a quiet life. … He's a romantic, and I'm more drawn towards a primitive condition.' Paul Gauguin to Emile Bernard, Arles, second half of November 1888, Merlhès 1984, p. 284.

19 Letter 663, to Theo van Gogh, Arles, 18 August 1888.

20 Letter 667, to Willemien van Gogh, Arles, 21 or 22 August 1888.

21 Purchased by the French State at Daubigny's studio sale.

22 Letter 590, to Willemien van Gogh, Arles, on or about 30 March 1888.

23 Van Gogh owned a great many prints with this motif, some of which formed triptychs, and his notion of combining paintings of trees in blossom to create a decorative scheme of triptychs and pendants (letter 597) may have been suggested in part by Japanese prints. It is more likely, however, that Van Gogh came up with the idea when he saw the sketches of the decoration of Emile Bernard's studio that the artist sent him (see letters 596 and 696).

24 Millet's *Spring* (1868–73, Musée d'Orsay) hung at the Millet exhibition of 1887 and was gifted to the Louvre the same year.

25 RM21, unsent letter to J.J. Isaäcson, Auvers-sur-Oise, 25 May 1890. César de Cock (1823–1904) was a Belgian landscape painter who worked with Corot in Barbizon in the 1850s and was greatly admired in his day. His work was sold by Goupil's; Van Gogh had met him at the Paris branch in 1873 (letter 17).

26 See the first essay by Lynne Ambrosini in this volume.

27 Letter 596, to Emile Bernard, Arles, on or about 12 April 1888.

28 Letter 666, to Theo van Gogh, Arles, 21 or 22 August 1888.

29 Letter 777, to Theo van Gogh, Saint-Rémy, between around Friday, 31 May and around Thursday, 6 June 1889.

30 Theo had written to him about Gachet as a friend of Pissarro's and other Impressionists; from the correspondence it does not appear that Vincent knew before he arrived in Auvers that the earlier generation of painters had also worked there.

31 For Daubigny and Auvers see the essay by Frances Fowle in this volume.

32 Letter 873, to Theo van Gogh and Jo van Gogh-Bonger, Auvers, 20 May 1890, and letter 874, to Theo van Gogh and Jo van Gogh-Bonger, on or about 21 May 1890.

33 Letter 875, to Theo van Gogh and Jo van Gogh-Bonger, Auvers, 25 May 1890.

34 See letter 873.

35 Letter 887, to Theo van Gogh, Auvers, 14 June 1890, and letter 889, to Theo van Gogh, Auvers, 17 June 1890.

36 For the scientific examination of the material of the 'double squares', which were all cut from the same roll, see Hendriks *et al.* 2013.

37 'The panoramic cycle of Auvers', in Zimmer 2009, pp. 111–14.

38 Another possible source of inspiration was the painting by Puvis de Chavannes that Van Gogh had seen at the Salon in Paris shortly before he went to Auvers, *Inter Artes et Naturam*, a wide landscape with figures that had deeply impressed him. See letters 879 and 893.

39 Letter 898, to Theo van Gogh and Jo van Gogh-Bonger, Auvers, on or about 10 July 1890.

40 Letter 891, to Theo van Gogh, Auvers, 24 June 1890.

41 Letter 898, to Theo van Gogh and Jo van Gogh-Bonger, Auvers, on or about 10 July 1890.

42 For Daubigny's studio see the essay by Frances Fowle in this volume.

43 Letter 889, to Theo van Gogh, Auvers, 17 June 1890.

44 Letter 902, to Theo van Gogh, Auvers, 23 July 1890.

45 Letter 898, to Theo van Gogh and Jo van Gogh-Bonger, Auvers, on or about 10 July 1890.

'TOUT DANS SON TALENT EST PRIME-SAUTIER, SAIN, OUVERT': OBSERVATIONS ON DAUBIGNY'S LATE PAINTING TECHNIQUES
René Boitelle
pp. 131–51

I would like to acknowledge the J. Paul Getty Museum's Paintings Conservation Council, Mark Leonard and Yvonne Szafran, for allowing me to spend two separate Guest Conservatorships in the Getty Paintings Conservation Department in 2007 and 2012–13. During this time I was able to continue my in-depth study of Daubigny's painting techniques while working on two of his Mesdag Collection paintings, *Cliffs near Villerville* and *Towpath on the Banks of the Oise*. I also thank those colleagues in other institutions, especially Marcia Steele at Cleveland Museum of Art, and Judith Dolkart and Carolyn Tomkiewicz at the Brooklyn Museum (2007), for inviting me to examine more Daubigny paintings and for allowing me to make references to works in their care. Analysis of paint samples of the two paintings from The Mesdag Collection was undertaken by Alan Phenix, Getty Conservation Institute, for which I am very grateful. Discussions with him on these complex samples provided an essential basis for my understanding of Daubigny's painting materials in the later stages of his career. I am also indebted to Devi Ormond for her insightful comments on an earlier version of this article, which were offered with a welcome combination of candour and warm humour.

1   'He is naturally spontaneous, robust, outgoing …' Henriet 1875, p. 42.

2   Moreau-Nélaton 1925, p. 81.

3   Keith and White 2002; Ortner 2014.

4   Hendrik Willem Mesdag was a great admirer of Daubigny's work. He assembled a group of paintings and drawings on which Moreau-Nélaton commented with great enthusiasm. In 1903, when the main body of the collection became the property of the Dutch state, the inventory included – among others – 13 canvases, 7 panels and 5 drawings by Daubigny. See Moreau-Nélaton 1925, p. 126 and figs 101–6. All paintings mentioned in this study are part of The Mesdag Collection, unless stated otherwise.

5   This series of standardised supports, introduced by the colourmen for their own convenience, was generally accepted and used throughout the century with slight alterations in height and width. By request artists could order non-standard sizes, prepared or unprepared and pre-stretched supports for specific purposes or commissions. See Callen 2000, pp. 15–19; Labreuche 2011. A review of the wooden supports of Daubigny's paintings from 1847 until 1877 reveals a strong preference for 38–9 (height) × 66–8 (width) cm.

6   The standardisation of wooden supports was not as widespread and generally accepted as that for pre-stretched canvases. Instead, the former seems to have been much more linked to the practice of individual manufacturers.

7   Alexis Ottoz, who came from a well-known family of Parisian colourmen, was in business between 1867 and 1874 at 46 rue Notre-Dame-de-Lorette, next door to no. 44, where Daubigny had a studio from 1870 onwards. See Constantin 2001, p. 65; Bomford *et al.* 1990, p. 43.

8   This painting is by far the largest of the versions known today that Daubigny painted of this subject in the 1870s.

9   The *Sunset near Villerville* may have been painted on top of another composition, although this could not be confirmed. The unprimed and unpainted fold-over edge along the bottom side and the position of the original crossbars suggest that the original support must have had a rectangular or even a double-square format (for example a standard-size *marine* no. 120; 97 × 194 cm). It is probable, though not certain, that Daubigny continued to work on the painting after adjusting its size. The slightly discoloured brushstrokes visible at the meeting of the original crossbars are clearly later additions, and were applied with greater artistic liberty than would be found in the work of restorers at The Mesdag Collection. At the most recent restoration (2005), they were not removed but somewhat toned down by retouching.

10 As a stamp at the reverse side indicates, the canvas came from the shop of Alexis Ottoz.

11 Letter to Adolphe-Victor Geoffroy-Dechaume, 23 [June 1854], cited in Moreau-Nélaton 1925, p. 62.

12 Letter to Frédéric Henriet, Paris, 30 September 1872, cited in Moreau-Nélaton 1925, p. 110. In academic tradition a *pochade* is a sketchy version of the *tableau fini* painted on a portable format *en plein air*, capturing the colours and atmosphere of the motif without too much detail. It is considered an object in itself, not an underpainting, created during the preliminary stages of the painting

process prior to composing a *tableau fini*. The measurements of the landscapes referred to in Daubigny's letter, which remain unidentified, probably concern the width of the canvases. At the final stage of his career, Daubigny may have intended to keep the *pochades* as they were, or to rework them later.

13 Oil on canvas, 54.5 × 166.2 cm, signed and dated lower right (Cleveland Museum of Art, 1951.323). The height is linked to a standard-size *paysage* no. 20, the width to a *portrait* or *paysage* no. 50. The pinkish ground was applied after stretching, probably by the artist himself.

14 Henriet 1875, p. 45, confirms that Daubigny prepared his own canvases and panels in the studio, regardless of the time it took.

15 Paint samples taken from *Cliffs at Villerville* and *Towpath on the Banks of the Oise* were mounted as cross sections and examined with optical microscopy (visual light and UV fluorescence) and Environmental Electron Microscopy with Energy-Dispersive X-ray Spectroscopy (ESEM-EDS). Selected spots of the paint surface of both paintings were also examined with X-ray Fluorescence Spectroscopy (XRF). Analysis of the ground layer in these samples has shown the presence of various mixtures of lead white, barium sulphate and chalk-based extenders. In some cases small particles of yellow/brown ochre were also found.

16 Standard-size *paysage* no. 15.

17 See for example *Apple Orchard*, probably created after 1872. Oil on canvas, 130.2 × 162.6 cm (Brooklyn Museum of Art, 02.252). The height matches one side of a standard-size *portrait* or *paysage* no. 60; the width that of a *portrait* or *paysage* no. 100. IR-reflectography revealed among other things that this painting, when it was already well advanced, was signed in the lower right corner, but at some stage this was covered by the artist with hatchings of opaque bright green paint that match the grassy foreground.

18 Standard-size *portrait* no. 20. See Boitelle and Van der Elst 1999, pp. 156–7, fig. 1 and pl. 31. The portrait was turned 90 degrees to the right before the night scene was painted on top.

19 The use of greens and blues in the *ébauche* stage of painting visible in *Towpath on the Banks of the Oise* has been linked to K. Robert's recommendations (first published 1878) on setting up a landscape painting, as well as to the practice of Monet and other Impressionist painters in the 1870s. See House 1986, p. 63 and pl. 103. The river scene was painted on top of an already existing but equally unfinished night scene. Regardless of whether the dark brown underlayer visible beneath the trees at the right was deliberately added when setting up the river scene or whether it belonged to the earlier painted night scene, Daubigny here combines two methods – the practice of previous decades which involved the use of earth colours in underlayers, with the innovative application of greens and blues as underlayers in other parts of the river scene, the range of which would be closely linked to that of the intended finished painting.

20 Present location unknown. Other versions of the subject (in which the farmhouses are mirrored) are a watercolour at the Metropolitan Museum of Art (*c*. 1860, 16 × 29.4 cm, 24.66.2) and a drawing at the Rijksmuseum (1865, 17.7 × 30.4 cm, RP-T-1948-535).

21 Henriet 1875, p. 43. Because of this claim, the painting has been cited as a key work in the history of Impressionism. See Bomford *et al*. 1990, p. 22; House 1995, no. 6.

22 Henriet 1875, p. 43.

23 The pigments identified in the samples are: lead white, zinc white, barium sulphate, ultramarine, cobalt blue, Prussian blue, emerald green, viridian, red and yellow iron oxide earth(s), cadmium yellow, chrome yellow, Naples yellow, vermilion, bone or ivory black, a starch- and aluminium-based red lake, yellow and yellow-brown lakes and a calcium-based extender. On the use of blue, yellow and green pigments by Daubigny and his contemporaries, see Burmester and Denk 1999. Note that scientific analyses performed at the time did not confirm the use of Prussian blue by Daubigny, but that this has been established by subsequent analyses, see Ortner 2014, p. 69.

24 Similar unconventional use of bright colours in irregular patterns, apparently independent of the final composition painted on top, has also been observed in *Moonlight* (The Mesdag Collection) and *Apple Orchard* (Brooklyn Museum of Art).

25 One critic stated that virtuoso brushwork as seen in the works of Old Masters such as Velázquez and Frans Hals should never be promoted and used to hide what is in fact sloppy technique and lack of talent, seen in works of some contemporary artists. Cottier 1875, p. 294. One year later another critic, discussing a *Lever de Lune* shown in London in 1874, defended the artist's paint application and compared it to that of the great Constable: 'What does it matter that they [Constable and Daubigny] brush their canvases like the devil, that they cover them with thick impastoed islands with the daring of masons at work; both arrive at the same effect ...' Lafenestre 1874, p. 25. It is tempting to speculate that Daubigny saw some of Constable's landscapes during his visits to London in 1866 and 1870–1. Two of the daring and innovative full-scale sketches of 'Six-Footers', *The Hay Wain* (1821) and *The Leaping Horse* (1825), already admired by Troyon when he saw them before 1853, were almost permanently on display at the South Kensington Museum from 1862 onwards. On Constable's innovative paint application in these large-scale sketches, see Cove 2006.

26 In reference to one of the paintings Daubigny presented at a Salon, Cham [Amédée-Charles-Henri comte de Noé] sketched a blurry image with two little figures and the comment: '... two unfortunate pedestrians walking in impastoed colours. They ask to be put back on the pavement as soon as possible.' Musée du Louvre, Département des Arts Graphiques, RF 39025 recto.

27 The remark was recorded by the American painter Dwight W. Tryon, who met Daubigny in 1877 and received some informal training from him in the artist's studio in rue Notre-Dame-de-Lorette. Hoeber 1915, p. 269.

Bibliography

Daubigny's life and work have received less attention than one might expect. Although his critical role vis-à-vis Impressionism was widely acknowledged in his lifetime, it was soon forgotten. After Frédéric Henriet's nineteenth-century publications and Jean Laran's volume on Daubigny in 1912, no significant publications were devoted to him between 1925, the year of Etienne Moreau-Nélaton's fundamental account, and 1975, when the important monograph by Madeleine Fidell-Beaufort and Janine Bailly-Herzberg appeared.[1] In 1976 Robert Hellebranth published a summary catalogue raisonné, arranged by geography of the painter's pictured sites; this was followed by a supplement in 1996. However, many facets of Daubigny's work and influence remain to be scrutinised, a fact that has further motivated this project. Indeed, a number of previously untapped archival sources on the artist have been consulted in researching the present publication.

Within the realm of museum exhibitions, Daubigny has also received surprisingly little attention. As Richard Brettell remarked in 1991, no internationally significant exhibition has ever been devoted to Daubigny – a fact that has remained true until now, twenty-five years later.[2] While exhibitions that surveyed mid-nineteenth-century French landscape as a whole have typically included Daubigny – see Herbert 1962, Clarke 1986, Loyrette and Tinterow 1994, and Brettell 2000 – monographic exhibitions devoted to him have been few and far between. Four modest shows have been mounted in Europe. The first two were commercial exhibitions: Hazlitt Gallery (London, 1959) and Galerie Barbizon (Paris, 1971). A third, under the expert guidance of Fidell-Beaufort, was held in a suburban city hall outside Paris (Aulnay-sous-Bois, 1990). The fourth was the inaugural exhibition of the charming Musée Daubigny (Auvers-sur-Oise, 2000). The only American efforts, quite restricted in scope and documentation, occurred fifty-two and thirty-eight years ago: at the Paine Art Center (Oshkosh, Wisconsin, 1964) and Dixon Gallery and Gardens (Memphis, Tennessee, 1978). It is high time, then, that Daubigny receives his moment on the international stage.

1 However, four academic dissertations from the second half of the twentieth century – Price 1967, Daguet 1971, Fidell 1974 and Grad 1977 – revealed increasing awareness of his importance.
2 Brettell, 'Foreword', in Champa 1991, p. 17.

ARCHIVAL SOURCES

Account Books (Musée d'Orsay)
Charles François Daubigny, Account Book (Livre de comptes), Département des Arts Graphiques, Musée d'Orsay, Paris

Account Books (Raskin-Daubigny)
Charles François Daubigny, Account Books, 1856–77, Raskin-Daubigny family, France

Durand-Ruel Archives
Archives Durand-Ruel. Stock Books of the firm Durand-Ruel & Cie; Archives of Impressionism, Paris

Frick Archives
Center for the History of Collecting at The Frick Collection and Frick Art Reference Library. The Archives Directory for the History of Collecting http://research.frick.org/directoryweb/home.php

Goupil Archives
Goupil & Cie/Boussod, Valadon & Cie Stock Books, Getty Research Institute, Los Angeles, http://www.getty.edu/research/tools/digital_collections/goupil_cie/index.html

Letters (Fondation Custodia)
Fondation Custodia/Collection Frits Lugt. Letters of Daubigny, Artists' Autographs Collection, Paris

Letters (Getty Research Institute)
Getty Research Institute. Letters of Daubigny, Archives Collection, Artists' Letters. Getty Research Institute, Los Angeles

Letters (Institut National d'Histoire de L'Art)
Institut National d'Histoire de L'Art. Collections Jacques Doucet. Letters of Daubigny, Artists' Autographs. Library of the Institut National d'Histoire de L'Art, Paris

Letters (Musée d'Orsay)
Charles François Daubigny, Letters. Copies of letters to Frédéric Henriet and other recipients made by Etienne Moreau-Nélaton. Department of Prints and Drawings, Musée d'Orsay, Paris

PUBLISHED SOURCES

About 1864
Edmond About, Salon de 1864, Paris, 1864

Aikema and Brown 2000
Bernard Aikema and Beverly Louise Brown, Renaissance Venice and the North: Crosscurrents in the Time of Bellini, Dürer, and Titian, Venice, 2000

Alexandre 1921
Arsène Alexandre, Claude Monet, Paris, 1921

Alexis 1971
Paul Alexis, 'Truble' – Auvers-sur-Oise', Le Cri du Peuple, 15 August 1887, reprinted in B.H. Bakker, 'Naturalisme pas mort': Lettres inédites de Paul Alexis à Emile Zola 1871–1900, Toronto and Buffalo, 1971, pp. 507–8, A:53

Ambrosini 2002
Lynne Ambrosini, 'Daubigny in Minnesota: Six Undeservedly Obscure Paintings', Gazette des Beaux-Arts, 6e pér., vol. CXXXIX, May/June 2002, pp. 395–412

Ambrosini 2012
Lynne Ambrosini, 'Mirrored Waters: Reflections on Monet and his Predecessors', in Benedict Leca, Monet in Giverny: Landscapes of Reflection, exh. cat., Cincinnati Art Museum, 2012, pp. 46–55

Amic 2013
Sylvain Amic (ed.), Eblouissants reflets. Cent chefs-d'oeuvre impressionnistes, exh. cat., Musée des Beaux-Arts de Rouen; Paris, 2013

Anderberg 2011
Birgitte Anderberg, French Art at Ordrupgaard: Complete Catalogue of Paintings, Sculptures, Pastels, Drawings, and Prints, Ostfildern, 2011

Anon. 1867
Anon., L'Album autobiographique: peinture, sculpture, architecture, l'art à Paris en 1867, Paris, 1867

Anon. 1868
Anon., Exposition maritime Internationale: journal officiel, Le Havre, 1868, nos 65, 170, 601–3, 679, 680

Anon. 1870
Anon., 'Lettre de Philadelphie', La Revue internationale de l'art et de la curiosité, 15 July 1870, pp. 75–6

Anon. 1873
Anon., 'Salon de 1873', Le Siècle, 11 May 1873, pp. 2–3

Anon. 1936
Anon., 'La Succession de M. Félix Rainbeaux', Beaux-Arts Magazine, 16 October 1936, p. 4

Anon. 1990
Anon., 'L'atelier de Daubigny: Le berceau de l'impressionnisme', La Gazette du Val d'Oise, 23 May 1990 [n.p.]

Assouline 2004
Pierre Assouline, Discovering Impressionism: The Life and Times of Paul Durand-Ruel, New York, 2004

Astruc 1859
Zacharie Astruc, Les 14 Stations du Salon, Paris, 1859

Auvray 1863
Louis Auvray, Exposition des Beaux-Arts, Salon de 1863, Paris, 1863

Auvray 1868
Louis Auvray, Exposition des Beaux-Arts. Salon de 1868, Paris, 1868

Bailly-Herzberg 1976
Janine Bailly-Herzberg, 'L'école de Barbizon; Rousseau, Daubigny et "petits maîtres"', Connaissance des Arts, no. 293, July 1976, pp. 80–2

Bakker 1986
Boudewijn Bakker, Monet in Holland, Amsterdam, 1986

Bakker and Van Dijk 2013
Nienke Bakker and Maite van Dijk, 'Van Gogh "in the country of paintings": an overview of his visits to museums and exhibitions', in Van Gogh's Studio Practice, Amsterdam and Brussels, 2013, pp. 56–77

Baranowski and Furlough 2001
Shelley Baranowski and Ellen Furlough, Being Elsewhere: Tourism, Consumer Culture, and Identity in Modern Europe and North America, Ann Arbor, 2001

Barrett 2010
Brian Dudley Barrett, Artists on the Edge: The Rise of Coastal Artists' Colonies, 1880–1920, Amsterdam, 2010

Barron 1889
Louis Barron, Les Fleuves de France: La Seine, Paris, 1889

Baudelaire 1968
Charles Baudelaire, Curiosités esthétiques et autres écrits sur l'art, ed. Julien Cain, Paris, 1968

Bazille 1992
Frédéric Bazille, Correspondance, selected by Didier Vatuone, ed. Guy Barral and Didier Vatuone, Montpellier, 1992

Belgrand and Lemoine 1877
Belgrand and Lemoine, 'Etude sur le régime des eaux du bassin de la Seine, pendant les crues du mois de Septembre, 1866', Annuaire de la Société météorologique de France, no. 25, 9 January 1877, pp. 3–80

Berson 1996
Ruth Berson, The New Painting: Impressionism 1874–1886, Documentation, Vol. 1, Reviews, San Francisco, 1996

Berson et al. 1989
Ruth Berson et al., The New Painting: Impressionism 1874–1886, exh. cat., Fine Arts Museums of San Francisco, San Francisco, 1989

Bertall 1853
Bertall [Charles-Albert d'Arnoux], 'Le Salon dépeint et dessiné par Bertall', Le Journal pour rire, no. 95, 21 July 1853, pp. 1–2

Billy 2002
André Billy, Les beaux jours de Barbizon, Etrépilly, 2002

Boime 1970
Albert Boime, 'Notes on Daubigny's Early Chronology', Art Bulletin, vol. LII, no. 2. June 1970, pp. 188–91

Boitelle and Van der Elst 1999
René Boitelle and Caroline van der Elst, 'A New Look at Old Definitions: Examining Notions of Finish in Barbizon School Landscapes', in Burmester et al. 1999, pp. 153–9

Bomford et al. 1990
David Bomford et al., Impressionism: Art in the Making, exh. cat, National Gallery, London; New Haven and London, 1990

Bonafoux 2008
Pascal Bonafoux, Correspondances impressionnistes, Paris, 2008

Bottin 1840–78
S. Bottin [aka Didot-Bottin], Annuaire-Almanach du Commerce de l'industrie, de la magistrature et de l'administration : ou almanach des 500.000 adresses de Paris, des départements et des pays étrangers, Paris, 1840–78

Bouillon 1986
Jean-Paul Bouillon, 'Sociétés d'artistes et institutions officielles dans la seconde moitié du XIXe siècle', *Romantisme*, no. 54, 1986, pp. 89–113

Bourguignon 2007
Katherine M. Bourguignon (ed.), *Giverny impressionniste: une colonie d'artistes 1885–1915*, exh. cat., Giverny and San Diego, 2007

Brenneman and Champa 1999
David Brenneman and Kermit Champa, *Monet and Bazille: A Collaboration*, exh. cat., High Museum of Art, Atlanta; New York, 1999

Brettell 1990
Richard R. Brettell, *Pissarro and Pontoise: The Painter in a Landscape*, New Haven and London, 1990

Brettell 1991
Richard R. Brettell, 'Foreword', in *The Rise of Landscape Painting in France: Corot to Monet*, ed. Kermit Champa, Manchester, NH, 1991, pp. 15–21

Brettell 1996
Richard R. Brettell, 'The River Seine: Subject and Symbol in Nineteenth-Century French Art and Literature', in *Impressionists on the Seine*, ed. Katherine Rothkopf *et al.*, Washington DC, 1996, pp. 87–129

Brettell 2000
Richard R. Brettell, *Impression: Painting Quickly in France, 1860–1890*, exh. cat., National Gallery, London, Van Gogh Museum, Amsterdam, and Sterling and Francine Clark Art Institute, Williamstown; New Haven and London, 2000

Brettell and Fonsmark 2005
Richard R. Brettell and Anne-Birgitte Fonsmark, *Gauguin and Impressionism*, exh. cat., Ordrupgaard, Copenhagen, and Kimbell Art Museum, Fort Worth, 2005

Brettell and Schaefer 1984
Richard R. Brettell and Scott Schaefer, *A Day in the Country: Impressionism and the French Landscape*, exh. cat., Los Angeles County Museum of Art, Art Institute of Chicago, and Grand Palais, Paris; New York, 1984

Brooke 1989
Janet M. Brooke, *Discerning Tastes: Montreal Collectors, 1880–1920*, exh. cat., Montreal Museum of Fine Arts, 1989

Brown 1991
David Blayney Brown, *Oil Sketches from Nature: Turner and his Contemporaries*, exh. cat., Tate Gallery, London, 1991

Burmester and Denk 1999
Andreas Burmester and Claudia Denk, 'Comment ils inventaient ces verts chatoyants?- Blau, Gelb, Grün und die Landschaftsmalerei von Barbizon', in Burmester *et al.* 1999, pp. 295–329

Burmester et al. 1999
Andreas Burmester et al., *Barbizon; Malerei der Natur—Natur der Malerei*, exh. cat., Bayerischen Staatsgemäldesammlungen, Doerner Institut and Zentralinstitut für Kunstgeschichte, Munich, 1999

Burty 1867
Philippe Burty, 'L'Hôtel des ventes et le commerce des tableaux', *Paris-Guide*, vol. 2, 1867, pp. 949–63

Busch 1980
Günther Busch, *Zurück zur Natur: die Künstlerkolonie von Barbizon*, exh. cat., Bremen Kunsthalle, Bremen, 1980

Callen 1982
Anthea Callen, *Techniques of the Impressionists*, Secaucus, NJ, 1982

Callen 2000
Anthea Callen, *The Art of Impressionism: Painting Technique and the Making of Modernity*, New Haven and London, 2000

Callen 2015
Anthea Callen, *The Work of Art: Plein-air Painting and Artistic Identity in Nineteenth-century France*, London, 2015

Cantrel 1863
Emile Cantrel, 'Salon de 1863', *L'Artiste*, no. 9, 1 May 1863, pp. 187–204

Castagnary 1861
Jules-Antoine Castagnary, *Salon de 1861: les artistes au XIXe siècle*, Paris, 1861

Castagnary 1864
Jules-Antoine Castagnary, 'Echos des ateliers', *Nouvelle Revue de Paris*, no. 1, February–March 1864, pp. 184–91

Castagnary 1874
Jules-Antoine Castagnary, 'L'Exposition du Boulevard des Capucines: Les Impressionnistes', *Le Siècle*, 29 April 1874, in Berson 1996, pp. 15–17

Castagnary 1892
Jules-Antoine Castagnary, *Salons (1857—1870)*, 2 vols, Paris, 1892

Chabanne 1990
Thierry Chabanne, *Les Salons caricaturaux*, Paris, 1990

Cham 1868
Cham, 'Salon de 1868', *Le Charivari*, 31 May 1868, pp. 1–2

Cham 1869
Cham, 'Paysage d'Alsace, effet de nuit', *Le Salon de 1869 charivarisé*, Paris, 1869, p. 13

Champa 1985
Kermit Champa, *Studies in Early Impressionism* (1973), New York, 1985

Champa 1991
Kermit Champa (ed.), *The Rise of Landscape Painting in France: Corot to Monet*, Manchester, NH, 1991

Champier 1878
Victor Champier, 'Nouvelles des Arts', *La Revue de France*, no. 28, March/April 1878, pp. 164–75

Chesneau 1868
Ernest Chesneau, 'Salon de 1868', *Le Constitutionnel*, no. 185, 1 July 1868, p. 1

Cheysson and Camère 1877
Cheysson and Camère, 'Débuts des eaux courantes … crue de 1876', *Annuaire de la Société météorologique de France*, no. 25, 9 January 1877, pp. 43–65

Chu 1992
Petra ten-Doesschate Chu, *Letters of Gustave Courbet*, Chicago and London, 1992

Claretie 1874
Jules Claretie, *Peintres et sculpteurs contemporains*, Paris, 1874

Claretie 1882–4
Jules Claretie, *Peintres et sculpteurs contemporains*, 2 vols, Paris, 1882–4

Clarke 1986
Michael Clarke, *Lighting up the Landscape: French Impressionism and its Origins*, exh. cat., National Galleries of Scotland, Edinburgh, 1986

Clarke 2003
Michael Clarke, 'Monet: Esquisse, Pochade', in Rapetti *et al.* 2003, pp. 129–133

Clarke and Thomson 2003
Michael Clarke and Richard Thomson, *Monet, the Seine and the Sea*, exh. cat., National Galleries of Scotland, Edinburgh, 2003

Clément 1864
Charles Clément, 'Le Salon de 1864', *Journal des débats*, 30 April 1864, pp. 1–2

Clément de Ris 1852
Louis Clément de Ris, 'Le Salon de 1852', *L'Artiste*, vol. 8, no. 5, 1 May 1852, pp. 98–104

Clément de Ris 1853
Louis Clément de Ris, 'Le Salon de 1853', *L'Artiste*, vol. 10, no. 5, 15 June 1853, pp. 145–9

Conisbee 1996
Philip Conisbee *et al.*, *In the Light of Italy: Corot and Early Open-Air Painting*, exh. cat., National Gallery of Art, Washington DC, 1996

Constantin 2001
Stéphanie Constantin, 'The Barbizon Painters: A Guide to Their Suppliers', *Studies in Conservation*, vol. 46, no. 1, 2001, pp. 49–67

Cottier 1875
Maurice Cottier, *Exposition Universelle de Vienne en 1873. Section française. Rapport sur les Beaux-Arts*, vol. 4, Paris, 1875

Courthion 1950
Pierre Courthion, *Courbet raconté par lui-même et par ses amis*, Geneva, 1950

Cousinié 2013
Frédéric Cousinié (ed.), *L'impressionnisme : du plein air au territoire*, Rouen and Le Havre, 2013

Coutagne et al. 2012
Coutagne et al., *Cézanne. Paris-Provence*, exh. cat., National Art Centre, Tokyo, 2012

Cove 2006
Sarah Cove, 'The Painting Techniques of Constable's "Six Footers"', in *Constable: The Great Landscapes*, exh. cat., Tate Britain, London, 2006, pp. 52–67; 203–7 (notes)

Curtis and Prouté 1968
Atherton Curtis and Paul Prouté, *Adolphe Appian, son oeuvre gravé et lithographié*, Paris, 1968

Daguet 1971
France Daguet, *Daubigny, 'Etude critique de la période 1870–1878'. Mémoire de Maîtrise*, MA thesis, Université de Paris I, Ecole du Louvre, Paris, 1971

Danchev 2012
Alex Danchev, *Cézanne: A Life*, London, 2012

Davies 1970
Martin Davies, *French School: Early 19th-Century*, National Gallery, London, 1970

De Calonne 1857
Alphonse De Calonne, 'Exposition des beaux-arts de 1857', *Revue contemporaine*, vol. 32, 1 July 1857, pp. 592–629

Défossez 1986
Marie-Paule Défossez, *Auvers ou le regard des peintres*, Saint-Ouen-l'Aumône, 1986

Delouche 1977
Denise Delouche, *Peintres de la Bretagne: découverte d'une province*, Paris, 1977

Delteil 1900
Loys Delteil, *Théophile Chauvel: catalogue raisonné de son oeuvre gravé*, Paris, 1900

Delteil 1921
Loys Delteil, *Le Peintre-graveur illustré, XIII, Charles-François Daubigny*, Paris, 1921

De Sault 1864
C. de Sault, 'Salon de 1864', *Le Temps*, no. 1159, 29 June 1864, pp. 1–2

Distel 1989
Anne Distel, *Les collectionneurs des impressionnistes, amateurs et marchands*, Düdingen/Guin, 1989

Distel 1990
Anne Distel, *Impressionism: The First Collectors*, New York, 1990

Distel and Stein 1999
Anne Distel and Susan A. Stein, *Cézanne to Van Gogh: The Collection of Doctor Gachet*, exh. cat., The Metropolitan Museum of Art, New York, 1999

Domergue 1954
René Domergue, 'Dans l'ombre de Cézanne et Van Gogh: Daubigny, Pissarro, Guillaumin et Constantin Guys', *Les Arts*, 3 December 1954, [n.p.]

Dorbec 1925
Prosper Dorbec, *L'art du paysage en France; essai sur son évolution de la fin du XVIIIe siècle à la fin du Second Empire*, Paris, 1925

Du Camp 1852
Maxime Du Camp, 'Salon de 1852', *Revue de Paris*, June 1852, pp. 125–49

Du Camp 1857
Maxime Du Camp, 'Salon de 1857', *Revue de Paris*, July 1857, pp. 161–224

Du Camp 1859
Maxime Du Camp, *Le Salon de 1859*, Paris, 1859

Du Camp 1863
Maxime Du Camp, 'Le Salon de 1863', *Revue des deux mondes*, vol. 45, no. 2, 12 June 1863, pp. 886–918

Dumas 1859
Alexandre Dumas, *L'Art et les artistes contemporains au Salon de 1859*, Paris, 1859

Duffy 2010
Michael Duffy, *The Influence of Charles-Francois Daubigny (1817–1878) on French Plein-Air Landscape Painting: Rustic Portrayals of Everyday Life in the Work of a Forerunner to Impressionism*, Lewiston, NY, 2010

Dupâquier 1985
Jacques Dupâquier, 'Corps et Ames: Les paysans du Vexin au début de la IIIe République', in *Le Monde paysan au XIXe siècle*, exh. cat., Musée Pissarro, Pontoise, 1985, [n.p.]

Du Pays 1852
A.J. Du Pays, 'Salon de 1852', *L'Illustration*, vol. 19, 26 June 1852, pp. 427–8

Du Pays 1857
A.J. Du Pays, 'Salon de 1857', *L'Illustration*, vol. 30, no. 761, 26 September 1857, pp. 202–4

Du Pays 1864
A.J. Du Pays, 'Salon de 1864', *L'Illustration*, vol. 44, no. 116, 16 September 1864, pp. 38–9

Duplessis 1856
Georges Duplessis, 'Les Marchands de tableaux; M. Adolphe Beugniet', *L'Artiste*, vol. 2, no. 6, 1856, pp. 290–1

Dupont 1855–9
Pierre Dupont, with preface by Charles Baudelaire, *Chants et Chansons (poésie et musique)*, 4 vols, Paris, 1855–9

Durand-Ruel 1939
Paul Durand-Ruel, 'Mémoires de Paul Durand-Ruel', in Venturi 1939a, vol. 2

Duret 1867
Théodore Duret, *Les Peintres français en 1867*, Paris, 1867

Duvergier de Hauranne 1873
Ernest Duvergier de Hauranne, 'Salon de 1873'. *La Revue des deux-mondes*, vol. 105, no. 2, May–June 1873, pp. 859–92

Duvivier 2007
Christophe Duvivier (ed.), *Les Peintres de l'Oise: Les Peintres-Graveurs de la Vallée de L'Oise*, exh. cat., Musée Tavet-Delacour, Pontoise, 2007

Eitner 1955
Lorenz Eitner, 'The Open Window and the Storm-tossed Boat: an Essay on the Iconography of Romanticism', *Art Bulletin*, vol. XXXVIII, 1955, pp. 281–90

Enault 1878
Louis Enault, *Les Beaux-Arts à L'Exposition universelle de 1878*, Paris, 1878

Fernandez 1997
Dominique Fernandez (ed.), *Le Musée d'Emile Zola: haines et passions*, Paris, 1997

Fidell 1974
Madeleine Fidell, *The Graphic Art of Charles-François Daubigny*, PhD dissertation, New York University, 1974

Fidell-Beaufort 2000
Madeleine Fidell-Beaufort, 'A Sketchbook by Daubigny: Traveling by Rail during the Reign of Louis-Philippe', *Master Drawings*, vol. 38, no. 1, Spring 2000, pp. 3–28

Fidell-Beaufort 2015
Madeleine Fidell-Beaufort, *Charles F. Daubigny: Drawings for Le Voyage en Bateau*, exh. cat., Jill Newhouse Gallery, New York, 2015 (published online at www.jillnewhouse.com)

Fidell-Beaufort and Bailly-Herzberg 1975
Madeleine Fidell-Beaufort and Janine Bailly-Herzberg, *Daubigny: la vie et l'oeuvre*, Paris, 1975

Fletcher and Helmreich 2011
Pamela Fletcher and Anne Helmreich (eds), *The Rise of the Modern Art Market in London, 1850–1939*, Manchester, 2011

Fletcher and Helmreich 2012
Pamela Fletcher and Anne Helmreich (eds), 'Local/Global: Mapping Nineteenth-Century London's Art Market', *Nineteenth-Century Art Worldwide*, vol. 11, no. 3, Autumn 2012, http://www.19thc-artworldwide.org/autumn12/fletcher-helmreich-mapping-the-london-art-market (accessed 1 July 2015)

Fournel 1859
Victor Fournel, 'Salon de 1859', *Le Correspondant*, vol. 11, June 1859, pp. 266–82

Fournel 1884
Victor Fournel, *Les artistes français contemporains. Peintres, sculpteurs*, Tours, 1884

Fourreau 1925
Armand Fourreau, *Berthe Morisot*, Paris, 1925

Fowle 2003
Frances Fowle, 'Painting like a Provençal: Cézanne, Van Gogh and the secret of Monticelli's "alchemy"', in Fowle and Thomson 2003, pp. 135–52

Fowle 2006
Frances Fowle, 'Making Money out of Monet: Marketing Monet in Britain, 1870–1905', in Frances Fowle (ed.), *Monet and French Landscape: Vétheuil and Normandy*, exh. cat., National Galleries of Scotland, 2006, pp. 141–55

Fowle 2013
Frances Fowle, 'Paysage sauvage, paysage moderne, paysage pittoresque: Monet et Guillaumin dans la vallée de la Creuse', in Cousinié 2013, pp. 187–98

Fowle and Thomson 2003
Frances Fowle and Richard Thomson (eds), *Soil and Stone: Impressionism, Urbanism, Environment*, London, 2003

Gachet 1990
Van Ryssel (alias Paul Gachet), 'De Daubigny à Van Gogh: Les artistes à Auvers', *L'Avenir de l'Ile de France*, December 1947, reproduced in Golbery 1990

Gachet 1956
Paul Gachet, *Deux Amis des impressionnistes – Le Dr Gachet et Murer*, Paris, 1956

Galerie Durand-Ruel 1845
Galerie Durand-Ruel, Paris, *Galerie Durand Ruel: Spécimens les plus brillants de l'école moderne*, 2 vols, Paris, 1845

Galerie Durand-Ruel 1878
Galerie Durand-Ruel, Paris, *Exposition rétrospective de tableaux et dessins des maîtres modernes*, Paris, 15 July–1 October 1878

Galerie Sedelmeyer 1889
Galerie Sedelmeyer, *Catalogue of the Celebrated Collection of Paintings by Modern and Old Masters and of Water Colors and Drawings Formed by Mr. E. Secrétan*. Paris, 1 July 1889

Gallet 1865
Louis Gallet, *Salon de 1865. Peinture, sculpture*, Paris, 1865

Gautier 1853
Théophile Gautier, 'Salon de 1853', *La Presse*, 23 July 1853, pp. 1–2

Gautier 1857
Théophile Gautier, 'Salon de 1857', *L'Artiste*, 2, no. 7, 25 October 1857, pp. 113–16

Gautier 1859
Théophile Gautier, *Le Moniteur universel*, 4 September 1859

Gautier 1861
Théophile Gautier, *Abécédaire du Salon de 1861*, Paris, 1861

Georgel 2007
Chantal Georgel, *La fôret de Fontainebleau: Un atelier grandeur nature*, exh. cat., Musée d'Orsay, Paris, 2007

Gill 1868
André Gill, 'Effet de lune – de Genève, huit trous en rubis, garantie 10 ans, par M. Daubigny', *Gill-Revue*, no. 1, 1868, p. 3–16

Godfroy 2000
Caroline Durand-Ruel Godfroy, 'Paul Durand-Ruel's Marketing Practices', *Van Gogh Museum Journal*, 2000, pp. 82–90

Golbery 1990
Roger Golbery, *Mon Oncle, Paul Gachet, Souvenirs d'Auvers-sur-Oise 1940–60*, Paris, 1990

Grad 1977
Bonnie L. Grad, *An Analysis of the Development of Daubigny's Naturalism Culminating in the Riverscape Period (1857–1870)*, PhD dissertation, University of Virginia, 1977; New York, 1977

Grangedor 1868
J. Grangedor, 'Le Salon de 1868', *Gazette des Beaux-Arts*, vol. 25, no.1, 1 July 1868, pp. 5–30

Green 1987
Nicholas Green, 'Dealing in Temperaments: Economic Transformation of the Artistic Field in France during the Second Half of the Nineteenth Century', *Art History*, vol. 10, no. 1, March 1987, pp. 59–78

Green 1990
Nicholas Green, *The Spectacle of Nature; Landscape and Bourgeois Culture in 19th-century France*, Manchester, 1990

Guégan et al. 1992
Stéphane Guégan et al., *Regards d'écrivains au Musée d'Orsay*, Paris, 1992

Harrison 1991
Jefferson C. Harrison, *The Chrysler Museum: Handbook of the European and American Collections: Selected Paintings, Sculpture, and Drawings*, Norfolk, VA, 1991

Haskell 1982
Francis Haskell, 'A Turk and his Pictures in Nineteenth-Century Paris', *Oxford Art Journal*, vol. 5, no. 1, 1982, pp. 40–7

Heilmann et al. 1996
Christoph Heilmann et al., *Corot, Courbet und die Maler von Barbizon: Les amis de la nature*, exh. cat., Haus der Kunst and Bayerische Staatsgemäldesammlungen, Munich, 1996

Hellebranth 1976
Robert Hellebranth, *Charles-François Daubigny, 1817–1878*, Morges, 1976

Hellebranth 1996
Robert and Anne Hellebranth, *Charles-François Daubigny, 1817–1878, Supplément*, [France: s.n.], 1996

Hendriks et al. 2013
Ella Hendriks et al., 'Automated Threadcount and the Studio Practice Project', in *Van Gogh's Studio Practice*, Amsterdam and Brussels, 2013, pp. 173–81

Henriet 1854
Frédéric Henriet, 'Le Musée des rues; Le marchand de tableaux [Beugniet]', *L'Artiste*, vol. 13, no. 5, 15 November 1854, pp. 113–15

Henriet 1857
Frédéric Henriet, 'Daubigny', *L'Artiste*, 5e sér. VII, 1857, pp. 179–82, 195–8

Henriet 1866
Frédéric Henriet, *Le paysagiste aux champs; croquis d'après nature*, Paris, 1866

Henriet 1874
Frédéric Henriet, 'Les paysagistes contemporains: Daubigny', *Gazette des Beaux-Arts*, 2e pér., vol. 9, 1874, pp. 255–70, 464–75

Henriet 1875
Frédéric Henriet, *Charles Daubigny et son oeuvre gravé*, Paris, 1875

Henriet 1876
Frédéric Henriet, *Le paysagiste aux champs*, rev. ed., Paris, 1876

Henriet 1881
Frédéric Henriet, 'C. Daubigny', *L'Art*, vol. 25, 1881, pp. 73–84

Henriet 1891
Frédéric Henriet, *Les campagnes d'un paysagiste*, Paris, 1891

Herbert 1962
Robert L. Herbert, *Barbizon Revisited*, exh. cat., Museum of Fine Arts, Boston, 1962

Herbert 1981
Robert L. Herbert, 'Industry in the Changing Landscape from Daubigny to Monet', in *French Cities in the Nineteenth Century*, ed. John M. Merriman, New York, 1981, pp. 139–64

Herbert 1988
Robert L. Herbert, *Impressionism: Art, Leisure, and Parisian Society*, New Haven and London, 1988

Herbert 1994
Robert L. Herbert, *Monet on the Normandy Coast: Tourism and Painting, 1867–1886*, New Haven and London, 1994

Herbert 2002
Robert L. Herbert, 'Industry in the Changing Landscape from Daubigny to Monet', in *From Millet to Léger: Essays in Social Art History*, New Haven and London, 2002, pp. 1–22

Hoeber 1915
Arthur Hoeber, *The Barbizon Painters: Being the Story of the Men of Thirty*, New York, 1915

Hôtel Drouot 1878
Hôtel Drouot, *Catalogue de la vente qui aura lieu par suite du décès de C.F. Daubigny*. Paris, 6 May 1878

Hôtel Drouot 1891
Hôtel Drouot, *Catalogue des tableaux et études par Charles Daubigny…Karl Daubigny … de Mme. Veuve Daubigny*, Paris, 14 April 1891

House 1978
John House, 'New material on Monet and Pissarro in London in 1870–71', *The Burlington Magazine*, vol. CXX, October 1978, pp. 636–42

House 1986
John House, *Monet: Nature into Art*, New Haven and London, 1986

House 1995
John House, *Impressions of France: Monet, Renoir, Pissarro, and their Rivals*, Museum of Fine Arts, Boston, 1995

House 2004
John House, *Impressionism: Paint and Politics*, New Haven and London, 2004

House et al. 2007
John House et al., *Impressionists by the Sea*, exh. cat., Royal Academy of Arts, London, 2007

Hubbard 1962
R.H. Hubbard, *Corot à Picasso: Peintures européennes dans les collections canadiennes* exh. cat., Galerie nationale du Canada, Ottawa, 1962

Huston 1990
Lorne Huston, 'Le Salon et les expositions d'art: réflexions à partir de l'expérience de Louis Martinet (1861–1865)', *Gazette des Beaux-Arts*, vol. 116, 6e pér., July–August 1990, pp. 45–50

Illyés 2001
Mária Illyés, *Oeuvres françaises du XIXe siècle*, exh. cat., Musée des Beaux-Arts, Budapest, 2001

Jacobs 1985
Michael Jacobs, *The Good and Simple Life: Artists' Colonies in Europe and America*, Oxford, 1985

Janin 1844
Jules Janin, *La Normandie*, Paris, 1844

Jansen, Luijten and Bakker 2009
Leo Jansen, Hans Luijten and Nienke Bakker (eds), *Vincent van Gogh – The Letters. The Complete Illustrated and Annotated Edition*, 6 vols, London and New York, 2009; www.vangoghletters.org

Jean-Aubry and Schmit 1968
Georges Jean-Aubry and Robert Schmit, *Eugène Boudin*, New York, 1968

Jensen 1994
Robert Jensen, *Marketing Modernism in Fin-de-Siècle Europe*, Princeton, 1994

Joanne 1856
Adolphe Joanne, *Les Environs de Paris Illustrés*, Paris, 1856

Johnston 1982
William R. Johnston, *The Nineteenth-Century Paintings in the Walters Art Gallery*. Baltimore, 1982

Jones et al. 2008
Kimberly Jones et al., *In the Forest of Fontainebleau: Painters and Photographers from Corot to Monet*, exh. cat., National Gallery of Art, Washington DC; New Haven and London, 2008

Joubert 1994
Alain Joubert et al., *La Seine: mémoire d'un fleuve*, Caudebec-en-Caux, 1994

Keith and White 2002
Larry Keith and Raymond White, 'Mixed Media in the Work of Charles-François Daubigny: Analysis and Implications for Conservation', *National Gallery Technical Bulletin*, vol. 23, 2002, pp. 42–8

Kelly 2013
Simon Kelly, 'Daubigny et Monet: le paysage de rivière, un produit commercial', in Amic 2013, pp. 34–41

Kelly and Watson 2013
Simon Kelly and April Watson, *Impressionist France: Visions of Nation from Le Gray to Monet*, exh. cat., Nelson-Atkins Museum of Art and Saint Louis Art Museum; New Haven and London, 2013

Labreuche 2011
Pascal Labreuche, *Paris, capitale de la toile à peindre XVIII–XIX siècle*, Paris, 2011

Lacambre 1974
Geneviève Lacambre, *Le Musée du Luxembourg en 1874*, exh. cat., Grand Palais, Paris, 1974

Lafenestre 1864
Georges Lafenestre, 'La Peinture et la sculpture au Salon de 1864', *Revue contemporaine*, vol. 39, no. 2, May–June 1864, pp. 342–69

Lafenestre 1874
M.G. Lafenestre, *Expositions Internationales. Londres 1874. France. Commission supérieure. Rapports*, Paris, 1874

La Fizelière 1864
Albert de La Fizelière, 'Salon de 1864', *L'Union des arts*, vol. 19, 4 June 1864, pp. 1–3

Lagrange 1864
Léon Lagrange, 'Le Salon de 1864', *Gazette des Beaux-Arts*, vol. 17, no. 1, 1 July 1864, pp. 5–44

Laran and Crémieux 1912
Jean Laran and Albert Crémieux, *Daubigny*, Paris, 1912

Lemaire 1986
Gérard-Georges Lemaire, *Esquisses en vue d'une histoire du Salon*, Paris, 1986

Lemoine 1976
Serge Lemoine, *La Donation Granville*, vol. 1, Dijon, 1976

Lépinois 1859
Eugène de Buchère de Lépinois, *L'Art dans la rue et l'art au salon*, Paris, 1859

Lochnan 2008
Katharine Lochnan, 'Whistler and Monet: Impressionism and Britain', in *James McNeill Whistler in Context: Essays from the Whistler Centenary Symposium*, Glasgow and Washington DC, 2008, pp. 45–64

London 1871
London, *International Exhibition of 1871, Official Catalogue. Fine Arts Department*. London, 1871

Lübbren 2001
Nina Lübbren, *Rural Artists' Colonies in Europe 1870–1910*, Manchester, 2001

Lublin 1993
Mary Lublin, *A Rare Elegance: The Paintings of Charles Sprague Pearce*, New York, 1993

Lucas 1979
George Lucas, *The Diary of George A. Lucas: An American Art Agent in Paris, 1857–1909*, introduction by Lilian M.C. Randall, 2 vols, Princeton, 1979

Mack 1951
Gerstle Mack, *Gustave Courbet*, New York, 1951

Mantz 1859
Paul Mantz, 'Salon de 1859', *Gazette des Beaux-Arts*, vol. 2, no. 1, 1 June 1859, pp. 274–99

Mantz 1873
Paul Mantz, 'Le Salon', *Le Temps*, 15 June 1873, pp. 1–2

Mantz 1878
Paul Mantz, 'Exposition universelle – La peinture française', *Gazette des Beaux-Arts*, vol. 18, no. 2, 1878, pp. 417–40

Marlais 2008
Michael Marlais, 'Daubigny, Courbet, and the Sluice Gate at Optevoz', in *Twenty-First Century Perspectives on Nineteenth-Century Art, Essays in Honor of Gabriel P. Weisberg*, ed. Petra ten-Doesschate Chu and Laurinda S. Dixon, Newark, NJ, 2008, pp. 110–15

Marlais et al. 2004
Michael Marlais et al., *Valenciennes, Daubigny, and the Origins of French Landscape Painting*, exh. cat., Mount Holyoke College Art Museum, South Hadley, MA, 2004

Mataigne 1985
Henry Mataigne, *Histoire de la paroisse et de la commune d'Auvers-sur-Oise. Depuis le commencement du IXème siècle jusqu'à nos jours*, Pontoise 1906; reprinted as *Histoire d'Auvers-sur-Oise*, Cergy 1985

Meignen 1996
Louis Meignen, *Histoire de la révolution industrielle et du développement, 1776–1914*, Paris, 1996

Melot 1980
Michel Melot, *Graphic Art of the Pre-Impressionists*, trans. Robert Erich Wolf, New York, 1980

Merlhès 1984
Victor Merlhès (ed.), *Correspondance de Paul Gauguin: Documents, Témoignages*, Paris, 1984

Merson 1861
Olivier Merson, *La Peinture en France. Exposition de 1861*, Paris, 1861

Merson 1873
Olivier Merson, 'Salon de 1873', *Le Monde Illustré*, vol. 33, 19 July 1873, pp. 39–42

Michel 1904
Emile Michel, 'A propos d'une lettre de Charles François Daubigny', *L'Art*, no. 782, December 1904, pp. 561–70

Millette 2004
Thomas L. Millette, 'An Ecological Reading of Daubigny's "The Water's Edge, Optevoz"', 2004 [ms in revision for publication, pp. 1–18]

Miquel 1975
Pierre Miquel, *Le Paysage français au XIXe siècle, 1824–1874*, vol. 3, Maurs-la-Jolie, 1975

Miquel 1994
Pierre Miquel, *Histoire des canaux, fleuves, et rivières de France*, Paris, 1994

Mitchell 1981
Peter Mitchell, *Jean Baptiste Antoine Guillemet, 1841–1918*, London, 1981

Moffett 1986
Charles S. Moffett, *The New Painting, Impressionism, 1874–1886*, San Francisco and Washington, 1986

Monneret 1994
Sophie Monneret, 'Daubigny et l'Atelier d'Auvers', in *Les Peintres d'Auvers: Daubigny, Cézanne, van Gogh*, special issue of *Beaux-Arts*, Paris, 1994, pp. 6–19

Moreau-Nélaton 1905
Etienne Moreau-Nélaton, *Histoire de Corot et de ses œuvres, d'après les documents recueillis par Alfred Robaut*, Paris, 1905

Moreau-Nélaton 1925
Etienne Moreau-Nélaton, *Daubigny raconté par lui-même*, Paris, 1925

Mouriez 1853
Paul Mouriez, 'Exposition de 1853', *L'Europe artiste*, no. 27, 7 August 1853, pp. 1–2

Museum der bildenden Künste 2003
Museum der bildenden Künste, *Von Corot bis Monet: Von Barbizon zum Impressionismus: Schenkung Bühler-Brockhaus an das Museum der bildenden Künste Leipzig*, exh. cat., Leipzig, 2003

Nochlin 1966
Linda Nochlin, *Realism and Tradition in Art, 1848–1900: Sources and Documents*, Englewood Cliffs, NJ, 1966

Nonne 2010
Monique Nonne, 'Alfred Cadart (1828–1875), marchand de tableaux modernes', *Bulletin de la Société de l'Histoire de l'Art français*, 2010, pp. 363–73

Nonne 2013
Monique Nonne, 'Le bateau-atelier', in Amic 2013, pp. 187–200

Ortner 2014
Eva Ortner, 'Die Schleuse im Tal von Optevoz – Ein Bild entsteht und wird verändert', in *Courbet > Daubigny: Das Rätsel der 'Schleuse im Tal von Optevoz'*, exh. cat., Bayerische Staatsgemäldesammlungen, Munich, 2014, pp. 63–97

Osborn and Bouvier 1856
Laughton Osborn and Pierre-Louis Bouvier, *Handbook of Young Artists and Amateurs in Oil Painting*, New York, 1856

Pantazzi 1996
Michael Pantazzi, 'Corot and His Collectors', in *Corot*, ed. Gary Tinterow et al., exh. cat., The Metropolitan Museum of Art, New York, 1996, pp. 397–405

Patry et al. 2014
Sylvie Patry et al., *Paul Durand-Ruel: Le Pari de l'impressionnisme*, exh. cat., Musée d'Orsay, Paris, 2014

Pelloquet 1858
Théodore Pelloquet, *Dictionnaire de poche des artistes contemporains: les peintres*, Paris, 1858

Perrier 1859
Charles Perrier, 'Le Salon de 1859', *Revue contemporaine*, vol. 9, no. 2, May/June 1859, pp. 302–3

Perrin 1859
Emile Perrin, 'Salon de 1859', *La Revue européenne*, vol. 3, 1 July 1859, pp. 655–6

Petit et al. 1899
Georges Petit et al., *Collection de M. le Comte Armand Doria, Tableaux Modernes*, 2 vols, Paris, 1899

Pickvance 1994
Ronald Pickvance, *Gauguin and the School of Pont-Aven*, London, 1994

Pissarro and Durand-Ruel Snollaerts 2005
Joachim Pissarro and Claire Durand-Ruel Snollaerts, *Pissarro: Catalogue critique des peintures*, 2 vols, Paris, 2005

Pomarède and Wallens 2002
Vincent Pomarède and Gérard de Wallens, *L'école de Barbizon: peindre en plein air avant l'impressionnisme*, exh. cat., Musée des Beaux-Arts, Lyon, 2002

Price 1967
Charles T. Price, *Naturalism and Convention in the Painting of Charles François Daubigny*, PhD dissertation, Yale University, New Haven, 1967

Privat 1865
Gonzague Privat, *Place aux jeunes ! Causeries critiques sur le Salon de 1865. Peinture. Sculpture. Gravure. Architecture*, Paris, 1865

Proust 1913
Antonin Proust, *Edouard Manet. Souvenirs*, Paris, 1913

Raffey 1869
Jacques Raffey, 'Galerie de M. Durand-Ruel', *Revue internationale de l'art et de la curiosité*, 15 July 1869, pp. 478–86

Rapetti et al. 2003
Rodolphe Rapetti et al., *Monet: Atti del convegno*, Treviso, 2003

Ravenel 1869a
Jean Ravenel, 'Exposition de Marseille', *Revue Internationale de l'Art et de la Curiosité*, 15 February 1869, pp. 116–29

Ravenel 1869b
Jean Ravenel, 'Exposition de Bordeaux', *Revue Internationale de l'Art et de la Curiosité*, 15 March 1869, pp. 253–59

Ravenel 1870
Jean Ravenel, 'Salon de 1870', *Revue Internationale de l'Art et de la Curiosité*, 15 May 1870, pp. 372–96

Redon 1986
Odilon Redon, 'Salon de 1868', in *Esquisses en vue d'une histoire du Salon*, ed. Gérard-Georges Lemaire, Paris, 1986, pp. 228–9

Reverdy 1973
Anne Reverdy, *L'école de Barbizon; Evolution du prix des tableaux de 1850 à 1960*, Paris and The Hague, 1973

Rewald 1946
John Rewald, *The History of Impressionism*, New York, 1946

Rewald 1973
John Rewald, *The History of Impressionism*, 4th ed., New York and Boston, 1973

Rewald et al. 1996
John Rewald et al., *The Paintings of Paul Cézanne. A Catalogue Raisonné*, New York, 1996

Robb 2007
Graham Robb, *The Discovery of France*, London, 2007

Rothkopf and Lloyd 2007
Katherine Rothkopf and Christopher Lloyd, *Pissarro: Creating the Impressionist Landscape*, exh. cat., The Baltimore Museum of Art; London, 2007

Rott 2014
Herbert Rott, 'Courbet, Daubigny, und die Schleuse im Tal von Optevoz', in *Courbet > Daubigny: Das Rätsel der 'Schleuse im Tal von Optevoz'*, exh. cat., Bayerische Staatsgemäldesammlungen, Munich, 2014, pp. 12–35

Rousseau 1857
Jean Rousseau, 'Salon de 1857', *Le Figaro*, no. 250, 9 July 1857, pp. 3–5

Roy 1999
Ashok Roy, 'Barbizon Painters: Tradition and Innovation in Artists' Materials', in Burmester et al 1999, pp. 330–42

Rózsa-Kaposy 1979
Veronika Rózsa-Kaposy, 'Madeleine Fidell-Beaufort – Janine Bailly-Herzberg: Daubigny' [on paintings by Daubigny at Budapest Museum of Fine Arts], *Acta Historiae Artium; Academiae Scientiarum Hungaricae* [Budapest], vol. XXV, 1979, pp. 169–73

Saglio 1860
E. Saglio, 'Exposition de Tableaux modernes dans la galerie Goupil', *Gazette des Beaux-Arts*, vol.7, no.1, 1 July 1860, pp. 46–52

Saint-Victor 1863
Paul de Saint-Victor, 'Salon de 1863', *La Presse*, 5 July 1863, p. 3

Saint-Victor 1864
Paul de Saint-Victor, 'Salon de 1864', *La Presse*, 26 June 1864, p. 3

Schulman 1995
Michel Schulman, *Frédéric Bazille 1841–1870, Catalogue raisonné: sa vie, son oeuvre, sa correspondance*, Paris, 1995

Sedelmeyer 1873
Charles Sedelmeyer, *Exposition Universelle de Vienne, 1873, France: Oeuvres d'Art et Manufactures nationales*, Paris, 1873

Shapiro 1985
Ann Louise Shapiro, *Housing the Poor of Paris, 1850–1902*, Madison, WI, 1985

Shiff 1984
Richard Shiff, *Cézanne and the End of Impressionism: A Study of the Theory, Technique, and Critical Evaluation of Modern Art*, Chicago, 1984

Shiff 2003
Richard Shiff, 'Monet and the Mark', in Rapetti et al., 2003, pp. 164–9

Shiff 2012
Richard Shiff, 'Sensation, Cézanne', in *Cézanne and the Past: Tradition and Creativity*, ed. Judit Geskó et al., exh. cat., Museum of Fine Arts, Budapest, 2012, pp. 33–47

Sillevis and Kraan 1985
John Sillevis and Hans Kraan, *The Barbizon School*, exh. cat., Haags Gemeente Museum, The Hague, 1985

Simon 1890
Jules Simon, 'Souvenirs de jeunesse', in P. Audebrand (ed.), *Faisons la chaine*, Paris, 1890

Société des artistes français 1857
Société des artistes français, *Explication des ouvrages de peinture, sculpture, architecture, gravure, et lithographie des artistes vivants exposés au Grand palais des Champs-Élysées*, Paris, 1857

Société des artistes français 1863
Société des artistes français, *Explication des ouvrages de peinture, sculpture, architecture, gravure, et lithographie des artistes vivants exposés au Salon de 1863*, Paris, 1863

Somers and Crnokrak
Agnès Somers and Catherine Crnokrak, *La Vallée du Sausseron: Auvers-sur-Oise, Val d'Oise*, Paris, 1992

Stein and Miller 2009
Susan A. Stein and Asher E. Miller (eds), *The Annenberg Collection: Masterpieces of Impressionism and Post-Impressionism*, The Metropolitan Museum of Art, New York, 2009

Stella 2001
Frank Stella, 'Grimm's Ecstasy', in *The Writings of Frank Stella. Die Schriften Frank Stellas*, ed. Franz-Joachim Verspohl, Cologne, 2001, pp. 147–51

Stolwijk 2003
Chris Stolwijk, 'Van Gogh's Nature', in *Vincent's Choice: Van Gogh's Musée Imaginaire*, ed. Chris Stolwijk, exh. cat., Amsterdam and Antwerp, 2003, pp. 25–43

Stop 1873
Stop [Louis Morel-Retz], 'Le Salon de 1873 par Stop', *Le Journal amusant*, no. 872, 17 May 1873, pp. 1–6

Talabardon and Gautier 2007
Talabardon and Gautier, *Le XIXe siècle, Exposition du 5 au 28 décembre 2007*, Paris, 2007

Tardieu 1857a
Alexandre Tardieu, 'Exposition de 1857', *Le Constitutionnel*, vol. 207, 26 July 1857, pp. 2–3

Tardieu 1857b
Alexandre Tardieu, 'Exposition de 1857', *Le Constitutionnel*, vol. 233, 21 August 1857, p. 3

Thompson 1993
Dodge Thompson, 'Charles Sprague Pearce: a forgotten realist of the gilded age', *The Magazine Antiques*, vol. 144, no. 5, 1993, pp. 682–4

Thomson 2000
Belinda Thomson, 'La nascita dell'impressionismo: dal Salon alla mostra degli indipendenti', in *La Nascita dell'Impressionismo*, ed. Marco Goldin et al., Conegliano, 2000, pp. 75–87

Thomson 1890
David Croal Thomson, *The Barbizon School of Painters*, New York, 1890

Thoré 1845
Théophile Thoré, *La recherche de la liberté*, Paris, 1845

Thoré 1847
Théophile Thoré, 'Par monts et par bois', *Le Constitutionnel*, 27 November 1847

Thoré 1870
Théophile Thoré, 'Exposition Internationale de Londres en 1862', in *Salons de W. Bürger, 1861 à 1868*, vol. 1, Paris, 1870, pp. 313–66

Thoré-Bürger 1870
Thoré-Bürger, *Salons de W. Bürger, 1861 à 1868*, Paris, 2 vols, 1870

Tillot 1852
Charles Tillot, 'Revue du Salon', *Le Siècle*, no. 6011, 2 June 1852, pp. 1–2

Tinterow and Loyrette 1994
Gary Tinterow and Henri Loyrette, *Origins of Impressionism*, exh. cat., Grand Palais, Paris, and The Metropolitan Museum of Art; Paris and New York, 1994

Tinterow et al. 2007
Gary Tinterow et al., *Masterpieces of European Painting, 1800–1920*, The Metropolitan Museum of Art, New York, 2007

Tryon 1896
Dwight W. Tryon, 'Charles François Daubigny', in John C. Van Dyke, *Modern French Masters: A Series of Biographical and Critical Reviews by American Artists*, London and New York, 1896, pp. 155–68

Tucker 1984
Paul Hayes Tucker, *Monet at Argenteuil*, New Haven and London, 1984

Tucker 1989
Paul Hayes Tucker, *Monet in the 90s: The Series Paintings*, exh. cat., Museum of Fine Arts, Boston; New Haven and London, 1989

Van Dijk et al. 2015
Maite van Dijk et al., *Hendrik Willem Mesdag; kunstenaar, verzamelaar, entrepreneur*, Bussum, 2015

Venturi 1936
Lionello Venturi, *Cézanne*, Paris, 1936

Venturi 1939a
Lionello Venturi (ed.), *Les Archives de l'impressionnisme*, 2 vols, Paris, 1939

Venturi 1939b
Lionello Venturi, *Camille Pissarro, son art, son oeuvre*, 2 vols, Paris, 1939

Viel-Castel 1853
H. de Viel-Castel, 'Salon de 1853', *L'Athenaeum français*, no. 26, 25 June 1853, pp. 607–9

Vose 1993
Robert C. Vose Jr., *Barbizon Returns to Vose: The Origins of Modern Painting*, exh. cat., Vose Galleries, Boston, 1993

Walter 1988
Rodolphe Walter, 'Aux sources de l'Impressionnisme: Bennecourt', *L'Oeil*, no. 393, April 1988, pp. 30–41

Watson 2008
Andrew McDonald Watson, 'James Duncan of Benmore, the First Owner of Renoir's *Bay of Naples (Morning)*', *Metropolitan Museum Journal*, vol. 43, 2008, pp. 195–200

Whiteley 2002
Linda Whiteley, 'L'école de Barbizon et les collectionneurs britanniques avant 1918', trans. André Fayot, in Pomarède and Wallens 2002, pp. 100–7

Whiteley 2014
Linda Whiteley, 'Brame, Hector', *Grove Art Online*, accessed through Oxford Art Online: http:/www.oxfordartonline.com:80/subscriber/article/grove/art/T010876 (accessed 3 April 2014)

Wickenden 1892
Robert J. Wickenden, 'Charles-François Daubigny', *Century Magazine*, vol. XLIV, no. 3, July 1892, pp. 323–37

Wild 1994
Barbara Wild, 'Charles Sedelmeyer: ein österreichischer Künsthändler macht Karriere in Paris', *Parnass*, vol. 15, no. 3, 1994, pp. 76–80

Wildenstein 1996
Daniel Wildenstein, *Monet or the Triumph of Impressionism*, 4 vols, Cologne, 1996

Wolff 1883
Albert Wolff, *Cent chefs-d'oeuvre des collections parisiennes*, Paris, 1883

Wolff 1886
Albert Wolff, *La Capitale de l'art*, Paris, 1886

Yriarte 1868
Charles Yriarte, 'L'Exposition finie…', *Le Monde Illustré*, vol. 22, 27 June 1868, pp. 401–3

Zacharie 1859
Astruc Zacharie, *Les 14 stations du Salon: suivies d'un récit douloureux*, Paris, 1859

Zimmer 2009
Nina Zimmer, 'Serial Van Gogh: cycles, groups, triptychs', in *Vincent van Gogh: Between Earth and Heaven, the Landscapes*, exh. cat., Basel 2009, pp. 96–117

Zola 1866
Emile Zola, *Mon salon*, Paris, 1866

Zola 1868
Emile Zola, 'Les naturalistes', *L'événement illustré*, 19 May 1868

Zola 1876
Emile Zola, 'Salon of 1876', *Les cahiers naturalistes*, http://www.cahiers-naturalistes.com/pages/Daubigny.html (accessed 11 April 2015)

Zola 1991
Emile Zola, 'Adieu d'un critique d'art', *L'Evénement*, 20 May 1866, reprinted in Zola, *Ecrits sur l'art*, ed. J.P. Leduc-Adine, Paris, 1991, consulted at http://www.cahiers-naturalistes.com/Salons/20-05-66.html (accessed 8 November 2014)

List of Exhibited Works

Charles François Daubigny
Landscape in the Roman Campagna, 1836 [fig. 1]
Oil on paper, mounted on canvas, 41 × 86 cm (16 ⅛ × 33 ⅞ in)
Brooklyn Museum, New York, Healy Purchase Fund B and gift
of Miss Isabel Shults, by exchange, 1991.214

Charles François Daubigny
The Crossroads of the Eagle's Nest, Forest of Fontainebleau,
1843–4 [fig. 2]
Oil on canvas, 89.5 × 116.2 cm (35 ¼ × 45 ¾ in)
Minneapolis Institute of Art, gift of Ruth and Bruce Dayton,
91.148.5

Charles François Daubigny
Landscape near Crémieu, c. 1849 [fig. 3]
Oil on canvas, 62.9 × 90.8 cm (24 ¾ × 35 ¾ in)
Minneapolis Institute of Art, gift of Mrs Peter Ffolliott, 79.59
Cincinnati only

Charles François Daubigny
The Harvest, 1851 [fig. 119]
Oil on canvas, 135 × 196 cm (53 ⅛ × 77 ⅛ in)
Musée d'Orsay, Paris, RF 1961

Charles François Daubigny
The Pond at Gylieu, 1853 [fig. 5]
Oil on canvas, 62.2 × 99.7 cm (24 ½ × 39 ¼ in)
Cincinnati Art Museum, gift of Emilie L. Heine in memory of Mr and
Mrs John Hauck, 1940.969
Cincinnati only

Charles François Daubigny
The River Seine at Mantes, c. 1856 [fig. 8]
Oil on canvas, 48.4 × 75.6 cm (19 × 29 ¾ in)
Brooklyn Museum, New York, gift of Cornelia E. and Jennie
A. Donnellon, 33.271

Charles François Daubigny
The Water's Edge, Optevoz, c. 1856 [fig. 7]
Oil on canvas, 66.7 × 122.6 cm (26 ¼ × 48 ¼ in)
Mount Holyoke College Art Museum, South Hadley, Massachusetts,
gift of anonymous donor in memory of Mildred and Robert Warren,
MH 1981.8
Cincinnati only

Charles François Daubigny
Spring, 1857 [fig. 73]
Oil on canvas, 96 × 193 cm (37 ¾ × 76 in)
Musée d'Orsay, Paris, on loan to the Musée des Beaux-Arts,
Chartres, RF 76

Charles François Daubigny
The Mill, 1857 [fig. 39]
Oil on canvas, 86.7 × 150.5 cm (34 ⅛ × 59 ¼ in)
Philadelphia Museum of Art, The William L. Elkins Collection,
1924, E1924-3-4

Charles François Daubigny
The Village of Gloton, 1857 [fig. 12]
Oil on panel, 29.8 × 53.7 cm (11 ¾ × 21 ⅛ in)
The Fine Arts Museums of San Francisco, Mildred Anna Williams
Collection, 1940.4

Charles François Daubigny
River Scene with Ducks, 1859 [fig. 62]
Oil on panel, 20.4 × 40 cm (8 × 15 ¾ in)
The National Gallery, London, NG 2622
Salting Bequest, 1910

Charles François Daubigny
Banks of the Oise, 1859 [fig. 54]
Oil on canvas, 88.5 × 182 cm (34 ⅞ × 71 ⅝ in)
Musée des Beaux-Arts, Bordeaux, BxE624

Charles François Daubigny
Landscape along a Country Road, 1860 [fig. 15]
Oil on panel, 20.2 × 33.8 cm (8 × 13 ¼ in)
Yale University Art Gallery, New Haven, gift of Miss Jessie M. Tilney,
in memory of her grandparents, John William and Hannah
M. Mason, 1938.23
Cincinnati only

Charles François Daubigny
Tugboat near Le Havre, c. 1860 [fig. 58]
Oil on board, 21.2 × 45.4 cm (8 ¼ × 17 ⅞ in)
The Art Institute of Chicago, bequest of Dr. John J. Ireland,
1968.89

Charles François Daubigny
Ferryboat near Bonnières-sur-Seine, 1861 [fig. 38]
Oil on canvas, 57.2 × 93.3 cm (22 ½ × 36 ¾ in)
Taft Museum of Art, Cincinnati, 1931.463

Charles François Daubigny
Banks of the Oise at Auvers, 1863 [fig. 77]
Oil on canvas, 88.9 × 161.3 cm (35 × 63 ½ in)
Saint Louis Art Museum, Friends Endowment and gift of Justina
G. Catlin in memory of her husband, Daniel Catlin, by exchange,
84:2007

Charles François Daubigny
Sunset on the Oise, c. 1865 [fig. 18]
Oil on panel, 23 × 33 cm (9 × 13 in)
Musée des Beaux-Arts, Dijon

Charles François Daubigny
Scene on the Thames, 1866 [fig. 43]
Oil on panel, 26.7 × 45.5 cm (10 ½ × 17 ⅞ in)
Museum of Fine Arts of Lyon
Cincinnati only

Charles François Daubigny
Flood at Billancourt, 1866 [fig. 17]
Oil on canvas, 50 × 65 cm (19 ⅝ × 25 ⅝ in)
The Phillips Family Collection

Charles François Daubigny
Boats on the Thames, c. 1866–7 [fig. 155]
Oil on canvas, 40.8 × 67 cm (16 × 26 ⅜ in)
The Mesdag Collection, The Hague
Edinburgh and Amsterdam only

Charles François Daubigny
Seascape, Saint-Guénolé, Penmarc'h, Brittany, c. 1867 [fig. 21]
Oil on canvas, 84 × 146.5 cm (33 ⅛ × 57 ⅝ in)
The Barber Institute of Fine Arts, University of Birmingham,
No. 72.1
Edinburgh and Amsterdam only

Charles François Daubigny
French Coastal Scene, 1867–71 [fig. 20]
Oil on canvas, 46.5 × 81.2 cm (18 ¼ × 32 in)
Tweed Museum of Art, University of Minnesota, Duluth, gift of
George P. (Alice) Tweed, D53.x22
Cincinnati only

Charles François Daubigny
Bank of the Thames, c. 1868 [fig. 44]
Oil on panel, 31.7 × 54 cm (12 ½ × 21 ¼ in)
The Mesdag Collection, The Hague

Charles François Daubigny
View of Herblay, 1869 [not illustrated]
Oil on panel, 38.8 × 67.2 cm (15 ¼ × 26 ½ in)
Scottish National Gallery, Edinburgh, NG 1035

Charles François Daubigny
The Dunes at Camiers, 1871 [fig. 22]
Oil on canvas, 57.2 × 65.4 cm (22 ½ × 25 ¾ in)
Minneapolis Institute of Art, gift of Wheelock Whitney, Wheelock
Whitney III, Pennell Whitney Ballentine, Joseph Hixon Whitney, and
Benson Kelley Whitney in memory of Irene Hixon Whitney, 86.90

Charles François Daubigny
St Paul's from the Surrey Side, 1871–3 [fig. 45]
Oil on canvas, 44.5 × 81 cm (17 ½ × 31 ⅞ in)
The National Gallery, London, NG 2876
Presented by Friends of Mr J. C. T. Drucker, 1912

Charles François Daubigny
Cliffs near Villerville, 1864–72 [fig. 131]
Oil on canvas, 100 × 200 cm (39 ⅜ × 78 ¾ in)
The Mesdag Collection, The Hague

Charles François Daubigny
Mills at Dordrecht, Salon of 1872 [fig. 51]
Oil on canvas, 84.5 × 146 cm (33 ¼ × 57 ½ in)
Detroit Institute of Arts, gift of Mr and Mrs E. Raymond Field,
32.85

Charles François Daubigny
Villerville, 1872 [fig. 27]
Oil on panel, 39 × 66 cm (15 ⅜ × 26 in)
Private collection

Charles François Daubigny
The Beach at Villerville at Sunset, 1873 [fig. 26]
Oil on canvas, 76.8 × 141 cm (30 ¼ × 55 ½ in)
Chrysler Museum of Art, Norfolk, Virginia, gift of Walter P. Chrysler,
Jr, 71.635

Charles François Daubigny
Apple Blossoms, 1873 [fig. 100]
Oil on canvas, 58.7 × 84.8 cm (23 ⅛ × 33 ⅜ in)
The Metropolitan Museum of Art, New York, bequest of Collis
P. Huntington, 1900, 25.110.3
Edinburgh and Amsterdam only

Charles François Daubigny
Orchard in Blossom, 1874 [fig. 103]
Oil on canvas, 85 × 157 cm (33 ½ × 61 ¾ in)
Scottish National Gallery, Edinburgh, NG 2586

Charles François Daubigny
Sunset at Villerville, 1874 [fig. 130]
Oil on canvas, 84 × 147 cm (33 1/8 × 57 7/8 in)
The Mesdag Collection, The Hague

Charles François Daubigny
The Coming Storm, Early Spring, 1874 [fig. 23]
Oil on panel, 44.4 × 69.4 cm (17 1/2 × 27 3/8 in)
The Walters Art Museum, Baltimore, acquired by Henry Walters,
1887–1895, 37.163

Charles François Daubigny
Fields in the Month of June, 1874 [fig. 109]
Oil on canvas, 135 × 224 cm (53 × 88 in)
Herbert F. Johnson Museum of Art, Cornell University, Ithaca, New
York, gift of Louis V. Keeler, Class of 1911, and Mrs Keeler, 59.087
Edinburgh and Amsterdam only

Charles François Daubigny
Seascape, c. 1874 [fig. 25]
Oil on canvas, 47 × 81.9 cm (18 1/2 × 32 1/4 in)
Private collection

Charles François Daubigny
Moonrise, 1874–6 [fig. 30]
Oil on panel, 37.1 × 64.1 cm (14 5/8 × 25 1/4 in)
Tweed Museum of Art, University of Minnesota, Duluth, gift of
Howard Lyon, D57.x12
Cincinnati only

Charles François Daubigny
Moonlight, c. 1875 [fig. 136]
Oil on canvas, 65 × 48.8 cm (25 5/8 × 19 1/4 in)
The Mesdag Collection, The Hague
Edinburgh and Amsterdam only

Charles François Daubigny
Towpath on the Banks of the Oise, c. 1875 [fig. 134]
Oil on canvas, 89 × 184 cm (35 × 72 1/2 in)
The Mesdag Collection, The Hague
Edinburgh and Amsterdam only

Charles François Daubigny
Landscape by Moonlight, c. 1875 [fig. 29]
Oil on panel, 34 × 55.5 cm (13 3/8 × 21 7/8 in)
Museum de Fundatie, Zwolle and Heino / Wijhe

Charles François Daubigny
Landscape with a Sunlit Stream, by 1876 [fig. 28]
Oil on canvas, 63.8 × 47.9 cm (25 1/8 × 18 7/8 in)
The Metropolitan Museum of Art, New York, bequest of Martha
T. Fiske Collord, in memory of her first husband, Josiah M. Fiske,
1908, 08.136.4
Cincinnati only

Charles François Daubigny
Sunset near Villerville, c. 1876 [fig. 129]
Oil on canvas, 89 × 130 cm (35 × 51 1/8 in)
The Mesdag Collection, The Hague

Charles François Daubigny
Beach at Ebb Tide, c. 1876 [fig. 138]
Oil on panel, 35 × 55 cm (13 3/4 × 21 5/8 in)
Rijksmuseum, Amsterdam, gift of M.C., Baroness van Lynden-van
Pallandt, The Hague, SK-A-1867
Edinburgh and Amsterdam only

Charles François Daubigny
Auvers, Landscape with Plough, c. 1877 [not illustrated]
Oil on canvas, 46.5 × 81.5 cm (18 1/4 × 32 in)
Toledo Museum of Art, Ohio, purchased with funds from the
Florence Scott Libbey Bequest in Memory of her Father, Maurice
A. Scott, 2015.18
Cincinnati only

Charles François Daubigny
Moonrise at Auvers, also known as *The Return of the Flock*, 1877
[fig. 31]
Oil on canvas, 106.5 × 188 cm (41 7/8 × 74 in)
The Montreal Museum of Fine Arts, gift of Lady Drummond in
memory of her husband, Sir George A. Drummond

Charles François Daubigny
October, 1850–78 [fig. 111]
Oil on canvas, 87.5 × 160.5 cm (34 1/2 × 63 1/4 in)
Rijksmuseum, Amsterdam, gift of M.C., Baroness van Lynden-van
Pallandt, The Hague, SK-A-1868
Edinburgh and Amsterdam only

Charles François Daubigny
The Harvesters, undated [fig. 110]
Oil on canvas, 43.5 × 89 cm (17 1/8 × 35 in)
Museum Gouda

Claude Monet
The Shore at Sainte-Adresse, 1864 [fig. 35]
Oil on canvas, 40 × 73 cm (15 3/4 × 28 3/4 in)
Minneapolis Institute of Art, gift of Mr and Mrs Theodore Bennett,
53.13
Edinburgh and Amsterdam only

Claude Monet
La Pointe de la Hève, Sainte-Adresse, 1864 [fig. 34]
Oil on canvas, 41 × 73 cm (16 1/8 × 28 3/4 in)
The National Gallery, London, NG 6565
Edinburgh and Amsterdam only

Claude Monet
Towing a Boat, Honfleur, 1864 [fig. 36]
Oil on canvas, 55.2 × 82.1 cm (21 3/4 × 32 3/8 in)
Memorial Art Gallery of the University of Rochester, gift of Marie C.
and Joseph C. Wilson, 91.35
Cincinnati only

Claude Monet
A Seascape, Shipping by Moonlight, c. 1864 [not illustrated]
Oil on canvas, 60 × 73.8 cm (23 5/8 × 29 in)
Scottish National Gallery, Edinburgh, NG 2399
Edinburgh and Amsterdam only

Claude Monet
La Pointe de la Hève at Low Tide, 1865 [fig. 33]
Oil on canvas, 90.2 × 150.5 cm (35 1/2 × 59 1/4 in)
Kimbell Art Museum, Fort Worth, Texas, AP 1968.07
Cincinnati and Edinburgh only

Claude Monet
The Seine at Bougival, Evening, 1869 [fig. 19]
Oil on canvas, 60 × 73.3 cm (23 5/8 × 28 7/8 in)
Smith College Museum of Art, Northampton, Massachusetts,
purchased, SC 1946:4
Cincinnati only

Claude Monet
Green Park, London, 1870/1 [fig. 46]
Oil on canvas, 34.3 × 72.5 cm (13 1/2 × 28 1/2 in)
Philadelphia Museum of Art, purchased with the W. P. Wilstach
Fund, 1921, W1921-1-17
Cincinnati only

Claude Monet
Houses on the Achterzaan, 1871 [fig. 76]
Oil on canvas, 45.7 × 67 cm (18 × 26 3/8 in)
The Metropolitan Museum of Art, New York, Robert Lehman
Collection, 1975, 1975.1.196
Cincinnati only

Claude Monet
Windmills near Zaandam, 1871 [fig. 53]
Oil on canvas, 48.3 × 74.2 cm (19 × 29 1/4 in)
Van Gogh Museum, Amsterdam, purchased with support from
the BankGiro Lottery, Stichting Nationaal Fonds Kunstbezit, the
Ministry of Education, Culture and Science, the Mondriaan Fund,
Rembrandt Association, the VSB Foundation and the Vincent van
Gogh Foundation
Edinburgh and Amsterdam only

Claude Monet
A Mill near Zaandam, 1871 [fig. 50]
Oil on canvas, 42 × 73.5 cm (16 1/2 × 28 7/8 in)
Ashmolean Museum, University of Oxford, WA 1980.81
Edinburgh and Amsterdam only

Claude Monet
Autumn on the Seine, Argenteuil, 1873 [fig. 157]
Oil on canvas, 54.3 × 73.3 cm (21 3/8 × 28 7/8 in)
High Museum of Art, Atlanta, purchased with funds from the
Forward Arts Foundation, The Buisson Foundation, Eleanor
McDonald Storza Estate, Frances Cheney Boggs Estate, Katherine
John Murphy Foundation, and High Museum of Art Enhancement
Fund, 2000.205
Cincinnati only

Claude Monet
Spring (Fruit Trees in Bloom), 1873 [fig. 101]
Oil on canvas, 62.2 × 100.6 cm (24 1/2 × 39 5/8 in)
The Metropolitan Museum of Art, New York, bequest of Mary
Livingston Willard, 1926, 26.186.1
Edinburgh and Amsterdam only

Claude Monet
View of Amsterdam, 1874 [fig. 52]
Oil on canvas, 50.3 × 68.5 cm (19 3/4 × 27 in)
Van Gogh Museum, Amsterdam, purchased with support from
the BankGiro Lottery, Stichting Nationaal Fonds Kunstbezit, the
Ministry of Education, Culture and Science, the Mondriaan Fund,
Rembrandt Association, the VSB Foundation and the Vincent van
Gogh Foundation
Edinburgh and Amsterdam only

Claude Monet
The Studio Boat, 1874 [fig. 66]
Oil on canvas, 50.2 × 65.5 cm (19 3/4 × 25 3/4 in)
Kröller-Müller Museum, Otterlo
Edinburgh and Amsterdam only

Claude Monet
The Studio Boat, 1876 [fig. 67]
Oil on canvas, 54.5 × 65 cm (21 ½ × 25 ⅝ in)
Musée d'art et d'histoire, Neuchâtel

Claude Monet
The Seine at Lavacourt, 1880 [fig. 69]
Oil on canvas, 98.4 × 149.2 cm (38 ¾ × 58 ¾ in)
Dallas Museum of Art, Munger Fund, 1938.4.M
Edinburgh and Amsterdam only

Claude Monet
Sunset, 1880 [illustrated page 9]
Oil on canvas, 50 × 61.5 cm (19 ⅝ × 24 ¼ in)
Private collection
Edinburgh and Amsterdam only

Claude Monet
Sunset on the River Seine at Lavacourt, Winter Effect, 1880
[fig. 72]
Oil on canvas, 100 × 150 cm (39 ⅜ × 59 in)
Petit Palais, Musée des Beaux-Arts de la Ville de Paris
Edinburgh and Amsterdam only

Claude Monet
Field with Poppies, 1881 [fig. 108]
Oil on canvas, 60 × 81.5 cm (23 ⅝ × 32 ⅛ in)
Museum Boijmans Van Beuningen, Rotterdam, 2611 (MK)
Edinburgh and Amsterdam only

Claude Monet
Fishing Nets at Pourville, 1882 [fig. 156]
Oil on canvas, 60 × 81.5 cm (23 ⅝ × 32 ⅛ in)
Gemeentemuseum, The Hague, 0332007
Edinburgh and Amsterdam only

Berthe Morisot
Rosbras, 1866–7 [fig. 41]
Oil on canvas, 55 × 73 cm (21 ⅝ × 28 ¾ in)
Private collection, on loan to the Minnesota Marine Art Museum,
Winona
Edinburgh and Amsterdam only

Camille Pissarro
La Varenne-Saint-Hilaire, 1863 [fig. 120]
Oil on canvas, 49.6 × 74 cm (19 ½ × 29 ⅛ in)
Museum of Fine Arts, Budapest, 377.B
Edinburgh and Amsterdam only

Camille Pissarro
Banks of the Marne, 1864 [fig. 57]
Oil on canvas, 81.9 × 107.9 cm (32 ¼ × 42 ½ in)
Kelvingrove Art Gallery and Museum, Glasgow, 2934
Lent by Glasgow Life (Glasgow Museums) on behalf of Glasgow
City Council. Presented by the Trustees of the Hamilton Bequest,
1951.

Camille Pissarro
The Marne at Chennevières, 1864–5 [fig. 37]
Oil on canvas, 91.5 × 145.5 cm (36 × 57 ¼ in)
Scottish National Gallery, Edinburgh, NG 2098
Edinburgh and Amsterdam only

Camille Pissarro
Orchard in Bloom, Louveciennes, 1872 [fig. 11]
Oil on canvas, 45.1 × 54.9 cm (17 ¾ × 21 ⅝ in)
National Gallery of Art, Washington DC, Ailsa Mellon Bruce
Collection, 1970.17.51
Cincinnati only

Camille Pissarro
Banks of the Oise near Pontoise, 1873 [fig. 9]
Oil on canvas, 38.1 × 55.3 cm (15 × 21 ¾ in)
Indianapolis Museum of Art, James E. Roberts Fund, 40.252
Cincinnati only

Alfred Sisley
Village Street in Marlotte, 1866 [fig. 40]
Oil on canvas, 84.8 × 111.1 cm (33 ⅜ × 43 ¾ in)
Albright-Knox Art Gallery, Buffalo, 1956:1
Edinburgh and Amsterdam only

Alfred Sisley
View of the Thames: Charing Cross Bridge, 1874 [fig. 48]
Oil on canvas, 33 × 46 cm (13 × 18 ⅛ in)
Private collection, on loan to the National Gallery, London
Edinburgh only

Vincent van Gogh
Bank of the Seine, 1887 [not illustrated]
Oil on canvas, 32 × 46 cm (12 ⅝ × 18 ⅛ in)
Van Gogh Museum, Amsterdam (Vincent van Gogh Foundation)
Cincinnati and Edinburgh only

Vincent van Gogh
Orchard in Blossom, 1889 [fig. 104]
Oil on canvas, 73.2 × 93.1 cm (28 ⅞ × 36 ⅝ in)
Van Gogh Museum, Amsterdam (Vincent van Gogh Foundation)

Vincent van Gogh
Orchard in Blossom (Plum Trees), 1888 [fig. 105]
Oil on canvas, 54 × 65.2 cm (21 ¼ × 25 ⅝ in)
Scottish National Gallery, Edinburgh, NG 2217
Edinburgh only

Vincent van Gogh
The White Orchard, 1888 [fig. 106]
Oil on canvas, 60 × 81 cm (23 ⅝ × 31 ⅞ in)
Van Gogh Museum, Amsterdam (Vincent van Gogh Foundation)
Amsterdam only

Vincent van Gogh
Daubigny's Garden, 1890 [fig. 123]
Oil on canvas, 50 × 101.5 cm (19 ⅝ × 40 in)
Collection Rudolf Staechelin

Vincent van Gogh
Daubigny's Garden, 1890 [fig. 122]
Oil on canvas, 51 × 51.2 cm (20 ⅛ × 20 ⅛ in)
Van Gogh Museum, Amsterdam (Vincent van Gogh Foundation)
Amsterdam only

Vincent van Gogh
Poppy Field, Auvers-sur-Oise, 1890 [fig. 107]
Oil on canvas, 73 × 91.5 cm (28 ¾ × 36 in)
Gemeentemuseum, The Hague, 0332858
(Loan Cultural Heritage Agency of the Netherlands)
Edinburgh and Amsterdam only

Vincent van Gogh [fig. 116]
Wheatfield with Cornflowers, 1890
Oil on canvas, 60 × 81 cm (23 ⅝ × 31 ⅞ in)
Fondation Beyeler, Riehen / Basel, Beyeler collection
Edinburgh and Amsterdam only

Vincent van Gogh
Wheatfields with Reaper, Auvers, 1890 [fig. 115]
Oil on canvas, 73.6 × 93 cm (29 × 36 ⅝ in)
Toledo Museum of Art, Ohio, purchased with funds from the
Libbey Endowment, gift of Edward Drummond Libbey, 1935.4
Cincinnati only

Vincent van Gogh
Wheatfields after the Rain (The Plain of Auvers), 1890 [fig. 114]
Oil on canvas, 73.3 × 92.4 cm (28 ⅞ × 36 ⅜ in)
Carnegie Museum, Pittsburgh, acquired through the generosity of
the Sarah Mellon Scaife Family, 68.18
Cincinnati only

Vincent van Gogh
Wheatfield near Auvers, 1890 [fig. 113]
Oil on canvas, 50 × 101 cm (19 ⅝ × 39 ¾ in)
Österreichische Galerie Belvedere, Vienna
Edinburgh only

Vincent van Gogh
Farms near Auvers, 1890 [fig. 89]
Oil on canvas, 50.2 × 100.3 cm (19 ¾ × 39 ½ in)
Tate, London, bequeathed by C. Frank Stoop 1933, N04713
Edinburgh and Amsterdam only

Vincent van Gogh
Farmhouse, 1890 [not illustrated]
Oil on canvas, 38.9 × 46.4 cm (15 ⅜ × 18 ½ in)
Van Gogh Museum, Amsterdam (Vincent van Gogh Foundation)
Edinburgh only

Vincent van Gogh
Wheatfields under Thunderclouds, 1890 [fig. 112]
Oil on canvas, 50.9 × 101.3 cm (19 ¾ × 39 ¾ in)
Van Gogh Museum, Amsterdam (Vincent van Gogh Foundation)
Amsterdam only

Vincent van Gogh
Rain – Auvers, 1890 [fig. 117]
Oil on canvas, 50.3 × 100.2 cm (19 ¾ × 39 ½ in)
Amgueddfa Cymru – National Museum Wales
Edinburgh only

WORKS ON PAPER

The entire series of sixteen etchings for Daubigny's *Voyage en
bateau*, 1862 will be shown in Cincinnati, an extensive selection
will be shown in Amsterdam. The entire set of twenty-three transfer
drawings will be shown in Edinburgh only. [illustrated figs 59–65]

Charles François Daubigny, *Le Voyage en bateau*, 1862
Two versions of the frontispiece; 15 drawings for the narrative
prints (see full list below); 6 drawings for plates not included in
the final printed version:
1. Frontispiece
2. *Le déjeuner du départ à Asnières* – 'Lunch at Asnières
   Before Departing'

3. *L'emménagement au Bottin (Le mobilier du bateau)* – 'Moving into "Le Bottin" (The Ship's Furnishings)'
4. *L'Héritage de la voiture (Les enfants à la voiture)* – 'Taking over the Cart (Children with the Cart)'
5. *Le mousse tirant le cordeau (Le triage à la corde)* – 'Cabin Boy Hauling the Tow Rope (Hauling by Rope)'
6. *Avallant (Le déjeuner dans le bateau)* – 'Guzzling (Lunch on the Boat)'
7. *Le mot de cambronne (L'Apostrophe)* – 'The Slang Match'
8. *La recherche d'une auberge* – 'The Search for an Inn'
9. *Intérieur d'une auberge (Le corridor d'une auberge)* – 'Interior of an Inn (The Corridor of an Inn)'
10. *Voyage de nuit (La pêche au filet)* – 'Night Voyage (Net Fishing)'
11. *Le mousse à la pêche (La pêche à la ligne)* – 'The Cabin Boy Fishing (Line Fishing)'
12. *Le Bateau Atelier* – 'The Studio on the Boat'
13. *Les bateaux à vapeur (Gare aux vapeurs)* – 'The Steamboats (Watch Out for the Steamers)'
14. *Coucher à bord du bottin (La nuit en bateau)* – 'Bedding Down Aboard the Botin (Night on the Boat)'
15. *Réjouissances des poissons du Départ du mousse (Les poissons)* – 'Rejoicing of the Fish at the Departure of the Cabin Boy (The Fish)'
16. *Le départ (Le Retour)* – 'The Departure (The Return)'
17. *Le botin amarré sous un arbre* – 'The Botin Moored under a Tree'
18. *La chasse aux oiseaux: Le mousse faisant peur aux oiseaux* – 'Hunting for Birds: The Cabin Boy Scares the Birds'
19. *L'aviron cassé* – 'The Broken Oar'
20. *La Forge* – 'Stirring the Pot'
21. *La Grèle* – 'Gleaners in the Hail'
22. *L'avant du botin, avec une grenouille, précédé d'un autre bateau* – 'The bow of the Botin, with a Frog'

CINCINNATI ONLY

Charles François Daubigny, *Le Voyage en bateau*, 1862
Etchings on paper
All 50.8 × 40.6 or 50.8 × 41 cm (20 × 16 or 20 × 16 ⅛ in)
Varied impression sizes, each approx. 13 × 18 cm (5 × 7 in)
Nos 1–16: Collection of Sallie R. Wadsworth
No. 17: 'The Studio on the Boat': Private collection, Cincinnati

EDINBURGH ONLY

Charles François Daubigny, *Le Voyage en bateau*, 1862
Twenty-three drawings: Pen and ink on *papier calque* – various dimensions
Lent by kind permission of the Jill Newhouse Gallery, New York

Charles François Daubigny
Le Voyage en bateau, 1862
Album of 15 etchings, 44 × 31.7 cm (17 ⅜ × 12 ½ in)
Printed by Auguste Delâtre
Published by A. Cadart and F. Chevalier
The British Museum, London

Charles François Daubigny
Le Bateau Atelier, 1861
Etching and drypoint, printed on Japan paper,
12.7 × 18 cm (5 × 7 in) plate
The British Museum, London

EDINBURGH AND AMSTERDAM ONLY

Charles François Daubigny
Le Voyage en bateau, 1862
Album, 44 × 31.7 cm (17 ⅜ × 12 ½ in)
Printed by Auguste Delâtre
Published by A. Cadart and F. Chevalier
Van Gogh Museum, Amsterdam

AMSTERDAM ONLY

Charles François Daubigny
Le Voyage en bateau, 1862
Etchings on paper – various dimensions
13 etchings
Rijksmuseum, Amsterdam

Charles François Daubigny
Landscape, 1865–70
Black chalk on wove paper, 38 × 63.5 cm (15 × 25 in)
The Mesdag Collection, The Hague

Charles François Daubigny
The Landscape Painter in his Boat, 1866
Print, 11 × 14 cm (4 ⅜ × 5 ½ in)
Van Gogh Museum, Amsterdam

Charles François Daubigny
Flock of Sheep by Moonlight, 1859
Charcoal, pen, ink and opaque watercolour on paper,
23.2 × 51 cm (9 ⅛ × 20 ⅛ in)
Van Gogh Museum, Amsterdam

Charles François Daubigny
Le Voyage en bateau, 1862
5 drawings: pencil, pen and ink on paper – various dimensions
Musée du Louvre, Paris

157

CLAUDE MONET

Autumn on the Seine, Argenteuil, 1873
Oil on canvas, 54.3 × 73.3 cm
High Museum of Art, Atlanta

Contributors

DR LYNNE AMBROSINI

Lynne Ambrosini is Director of Collections and Exhibitions and Curator of European Art at the Taft Museum of Art, Cincinnati. Among the articles she has published are: 'Daubigny: Six Undeservedly Obscure Paintings', *Gazette des Beaux-Arts* (2002); 'Eyeing the Sculptural Nude: Public Response in the Early Modern Era', *Sculpture Review* (2008); and 'Mirrored Waters: Reflections on Monet and his Predecessors', in *Monet in Giverny*, Cincinnati Art Museum (2012). Her exhibitions for the Taft include *Hiram Powers: Genius in Marble* (2007), for which she co-authored the catalogue; *Brush, Clay, Wood: The Rosenthal Collection* (2008); and *American Impressionism from Cincinnati Collections* (2011).

NIENKE BAKKER

Nienke Bakker is Curator of Paintings at the Van Gogh Museum. She was one of the editors of *Vincent van Gogh, Painted with Words: The Letters to Emile Bernard* (2007); the web version of Van Gogh's complete correspondence, www.vangoghletters.org (2009); the six-volume *Vincent van Gogh – The Letters: The Complete Illustrated and Annotated Edition* (2009); and *Vincent van Gogh, Ever Yours: The Essential Letters* (2014). She has curated various exhibitions on Vincent van Gogh and late nineteenth-century art, among others *Van Gogh's Letters: The Artist Speaks* (2009), *Van Gogh at Work* (2013) and *Splendours and Miseries: Images of Prostitution in France, 1850–1910* (2015). She has contributed to scholarly publications and exhibition catalogues including *The Real Van Gogh: The Artist and His Letters* (2010); *Picasso in Paris* (2011); *Van Gogh's Studio Practice* (2013); and *Van Gogh–Artaud* (2014).

RENÉ BOITELLE

René Boitelle is Senior Paintings Conservator at the Van Gogh Museum. He received his degree in Art History from the University of Leiden then followed the Programme for the Conservation of Paintings and Polychrome Objects at SRAL, Maastricht. After a series of internships in various museums he became a paintings conservator at the Van Gogh Museum, where he specialises in the research and treatment of paintings by painters of the Barbizon School and by Van Gogh's contemporaries. Results of his research have found their way into articles on works by Millet, Daubigny, Rousseau, Gauguin, Bernard and Redon.

MICHAEL CLARKE

After holding curatorial posts in York, the British Museum and Manchester University, Michael Clarke joined the staff of the Scottish National Gallery in 1984 and has been Director since 2000. His numerous publications include monographs on British watercolours and Camille Corot, and *The Oxford Concise Dictionary of Art Terms*. Exhibitions he has curated include *Lighting up the Landscape: French Impressionism and its Origins* (1986); *Corot, Courbet und die Maler von Barbizon* (1996); *Monet: The Seine and the Sea* (2003); and *Poussin to Seurat: French Drawings in the Scottish National Gallery* (2010). He is currently working, with Frances Fowle, on the catalogue of all the French paintings in the Scottish National Gallery.

MAITE VAN DIJK

Maite van Dijk has been Curator of Paintings at the Van Gogh Museum since 2008, where she is responsible for the paintings by Van Gogh's contemporaries. She is also in charge of the nineteenth-century paintings collection at The Mesdag Collection, The Hague. In recent years she has curated the new installations of the permanent collection in both the Van Gogh Museum (2014) and The Mesdag Collection (2011), and she was in charge of the exhibition and catalogue *Munch: Van Gogh* (2015). She is currently directing the research for the collection catalogue on Van Gogh's contemporaries and finishing her dissertation on the critical reception of foreign artists at the Salon des Indépendants in Paris (1884–1914).

DR FRANCES FOWLE

Frances Fowle is Reader in History of Art at the University of Edinburgh and Senior Curator of French Art at the Scottish National Gallery. She has published widely and is the author of *Van Gogh's Twin: the Scottish Art Dealer Alexander Reid: 1854–1928* (2010). Edited books include *Soil and Stone: Impressionism, Urbanism, Environment* (2003) and *Monet and French Landscape: Vétheuil and Normandy* (2006). She has curated a number of exhibitions for the National Galleries of Scotland, notably *Van Gogh and Britain: Pioneer Collectors* (2006); *Impressionism and Scotland* (2008); *Van Gogh to Kandinsky: Symbolist Landscape in Europe 1880–1910* (2012); and *American Impressionism: A New Vision 1880–1900* (2014). She is currently working, with Michael Clarke, on the critical catalogue of the French paintings in the Scottish National Gallery.

Published by the Trustees of the National Galleries of Scotland
to accompany the following exhibitions:

Daubigny, Monet, Van Gogh: Impressions of Landscape
held at the Taft Museum of Art, Cincinnati
from 20 February 2016 to 29 May 2016.

Inspiring Impressionism: Daubigny, Monet, Van Gogh
held at the Scottish National Gallery, Edinburgh,
from 25 June 2016 to 2 October 2016.

Daubigny, Monet, Van Gogh: Impressions of Landscape
held at the Van Gogh Museum, Amsterdam
from 21 October 2016 to 29 January 2017.

Text © 2015 the Trustees of the National Galleries of Scotland
and the authors

Edition Taft Museum of Art, Cincinnati: ISBN 978-1-906270-95-7
Edition National Galleries of Scotland: ISBN 978-1-906270-86-5
Edition Van Gogh Museum, Amsterdam: ISBN 978-90-79310-57-9
(English)
Edition Van Gogh Museum, Amsterdam: ISBN 978-90-79310-58-6
(Dutch)

EXHIBITION

TAFT MUSEUM OF ART

Curator
Lynne Ambrosini

Curatorial Assistant
Katie G. Benedict

Registrar
Joan Hendricks

NATIONAL GALLERIES OF SCOTLAND

Curators
Michael Clarke, Frances Fowle

PA to the Director
Matt Ramagge

Registrars
Rosalyn Clancey, Louise Rowlands

VAN GOGH MUSEUM, AMSTERDAM

Curators
Nienke Bakker, Maite van Dijk

Registrar
Mechtild Beckers

Exhibition Management
Geeta Bruin

CATALOGUE

Editorial Board
Lynne Ambrosini, Frances Fowle, Maite van Dijk

NATIONAL GALLERIES OF SCOTLAND

Publishing Department
Christine Thompson

Picture Research
Gillian Achurch

English Translation Chapter 2 and 6
Lynne Richards

Copy-Editing
Kate Bell

VAN GOGH MUSEUM, AMSTERDAM

Publishing Department
Suzanne Bogman, Betty Klaasse

Production
Tijdsbeeld & Pièce Montée, Ghent –
Ronny Gobyn and Rik Jacques (directors)

Design
Janpieter Chielens, Tijdsbeeld & Pièce Montée

Typesetting
Yanne Devos, Tijdsbeeld & Pièce Montée

Coordination
Barbara Costermans, Tijdsgeest, Ghent

Print
Graphius, Ghent

Typeset in ITC Franklin Gothic and Scotch Roman MT
Paper Luxo Samt Art 150g

Front cover
Charles François Daubigny, *Sunset near Villerville*, c. 1876 [fig. 129]
The Mesdag Collection, The Hague

Back cover
Charles François Daubigny, *Orchard in Blossom*, 1874 [fig. 103]
Scottish National Gallery, Edinburgh

Claude Monet, *Spring (Fruit Trees in Bloom)*, 1873 [fig. 101]
The Metropolitan Museum of Art, New York

Vincent van Gogh, *The White Orchard*, 1888 [fig. 106]
Van Gogh Museum (Vincent van Gogh Foundation), Amsterdam

Back cover flap
Charles François Daubigny, *Apple Blossoms*, 1873 [fig. 100]
The Metropolitan Museum of Art, New York

Title page
Charles François Daubigny, *Moonrise at Auvers*, also known as
The Return of the Flock, 1877 [fig. 31]
The Montreal Museum of Fine Arts

Frontispiece
Vincent van Gogh, *Daubigny's Garden*, 1890 [fig. 123]
Collection Rudolf Staechelin

Copyright and Photographic Credits